SAMURAI, SHOGUNS, AND SOLDIERS:
THE RISE OF THE JAPANESE MILITARY

Titles in the series include:

From Painted Scrolls to Anime: Literature and the Arts of Japan
Shinto, Spirits, and Shrines: Religion in Japan
The War at Home: Japan during World War II
Up from the Ashes: Rebuilding Japan after World War II

SAMURAI, SHOGUNS, AND SOLDIERS: THE RISE OF THE JAPANESE MILITARY

BARBARA A. SOMERVILL

LUCENT BOOKS

An imprint of Thomson Gale, a part of The Thomson Corporation

THOMSON

——————★——————™

GALE

Detroit • New York • San Francisco • New Haven, Conn. • Waterville, Maine • London

For more information, contact
Lucent Books
27500 Drake Rd.
Farmington Hills, MI 48331-3535
Or you can visit our Internet site at http://www.gale.com

LIBRARY OF CONGRESS CATALOGING-IN-PUBLICATION DATA

Somervill, Barbara A.
  Samurai, Shoguns, and Soldiers : The Rise of the Japanese Military /
by Barbara A. Somervill.
     p. cm. -- (Lucent library of historical eras. Twentieth-century
Japan)
  Includes bibliographical references and index.
  ISBN 978-1-4205-0030-1 (hardcover)
  1. Japan--History, Military--Juvenile literature. I. Title.
  DS838.S66 2007
  952--dc22
                                                                2007030619

ISBN-10: 1-4205-0030-9
Printed in the United States of America

Contents

Foreword   6

Timeline   8

Introduction
Militarism in Japan   10

Chapter One
The Early Roots of Militarism   13

Chapter Two
The Meiji Restoration   27

Chapter Three
Times of Trouble   38

Chapter Four
Upheaval at Home and Abroad   51

Chapter Five
1936—A Pivotal Year   65

Chapter Six
The Storm Breaks   78

Notes   91

For Further Reading   93

Works Consulted   95

Index   97

Picture Credits   103

About the Author   104

Foreword

Looking back from the vantage point of the present, history can be viewed as a myriad of intertwining roads paved by human events. Some paths stand out—broad highways whose mileposts, even from a distance of centuries, are clear. The events that propelled the rise to power of Germany's Third Reich, its role in World War II, and its eventual demise, for example, are well defined and documented.

Other roads are less distinct, their route sometimes hidden from view. Modern legislatures may have developed from old tribal councils, for example, but the links between them are indistinct in places, open to discussion and interpretation.

The architecture of civilization—law, religion, art, science, and government—as well as the more everyday aspects of our culture—what we eat, what we wear—all developed along the historical roads and byways. In that progression can be traced every facet of modern life.

A broad look back along these roads reveals that many paths—though of vastly different character—seem to converge at a few critical junctions. These intersections are those great historical eras that echo over the long, steady course of human history, extending beyond the past and into the present.

These epic periods of time are the focus of Historical Eras. They shine through the mists of history like beacons, illuminated by a burst of creativity that propels events forward—so bright that we, from thousands of years away, can clearly see the chain of events leading to the present.

Each Historical Eras consists of a set of books that highlight various aspects of these major eras. For example, the Elizabethan England library features volumes on Queen Elizabeth I and her court, Elizabethan theater, the great playwrights, and everyday life in Elizabethan London.

The mini-library approach allows for the division of each era into its most significant and most interesting parts and the exploration of those parts in depth. Also, social and cultural trends as well as illustrative documents and eyewitness accounts can be prominently featured in individual volumes.

Historical Eras present a wealth of information to young readers. The lively narrative, fully documented primary and secondary source quotations, maps, photographs, sidebars, and annotated bibliographies serve as launching points for class discussion and further research.

In studying the great historical eras, students also develop a better understanding of our own times. What we learn from the past and how we apply it in the present may shape the future and may determine whether our era will be a guiding light to those traveling future roads.

Timeline

1180   Minamoto family takes control of Japan; Minamoto Yorimoto appointed first shogun

1338   Ashikaga Takauji appointed shogun; Muromachi period begins

1600   Tokugawa Ieyasu becomes shogun; Tokugawa era begins

1853   U.S. naval commodore Perry arrives in Japan to establish trading rights

1867   Group of samurai overthrows government; Emperor Meiji begins reign; Tokyo becomes capital

1873   Japan introduces conscription law; antidraft riots ensue

1877   The Satsuma Rebellion

1889   Meiji Constitution presented to Japan

1890   Imperial Diet meets for first time

1894–95   First Sino-Japanese War

1904–05   Russo-Japanese War

1910   Japan annexes Korea as a colony

1912   Emperor Meiji dies; Taisho era begins

1914–18   World War I

1915   Japan presents China with list of the Twenty-one Demands

1920   Japan becomes founding member of the League of Nations

1921	Hirohito appointed regent for his father	1931	The Manchurian Incident
1922	Japan signs the Five-Power Naval Arms Limitation Treaty	1936	The February 26 Incident; Japan and Germany sign the Anti-Comintern Pact
1923	The Great Kanto Earthquake destroys Tokyo and Yokohama	1937	The Marco Polo Bridge Incident; Second Sino-Japanese War begins
1926	Emperor Taisho dies; Hirohito becomes emperor; Showa era begins	1937–38	The Nanjing Massacre
1929	New York Stock Market crashes; the Great Depression begins	1938	Japan announces new order in East Asia

Introduction

MILITARISM IN JAPAN

Throughout history, military might has brought war and peace as well as prosperity and hardship to many nations. Militarism—the belief that a society is best governed by military leaders—increased in the twentieth century, but it was by no means a new idea.

Militarism came easily to Japan. The traditions of the Japanese warrior class stretch back as early as the eighth century when Emperor Mommu ordered that one in three adult males report for military service. It was from this early army of drafted men that the *samurai*, or warrior class of Japan, was born.

Through the centuries, though, the samurai became more than just an army. They came to be considered an elite social class. The samurai followed a strict code of honor that they described as *kyuba no michi*, which translates to "the way of the bow and horse." Their concept of *Bushido*, "the way of the warrior," equaled the code of chivalry lived by European knights. This code combined loyalty, military skills, an austere lifestyle, and honor to the death. As the centuries passed, though, samurai became more than just a collection of mercenary soldiers. Many were well educated. They still trained in the martial arts, but they began to study the fine arts as well. Some even began to write music and poetry. These professional warriors passed these skills down to their sons along with a sense of loyalty, commitment, service, and most important, honor.

Political power, too, was concentrated in the hands of the samurai class. Officially, Japan was governed by an emperor. In reality, the *shogun*, the country's highest military commander, made all government decisions with a staff of close advisers. This system of government lasted for almost seven hundred years, establishing a tradition of rule by military leaders.

By the mid-1800s, though, life in Japan was changing rapidly. The role of the samurai changed with it. Samurai gradually moved away from warrior status and became known as politicians, diplomats, courtiers, and managers. By 1853, when Commodore Matthew Perry of the United States Navy sailed into the Japanese waters of Tokyo Bay and insisted that Japan open its doors to foreign trade, the age of the shogun was coming to an end.

The unwanted interference from the outside world brought about changes in Japan that had far-reaching consequences. Even though Japan did enter into treaties with some Western nations, these treaties gave little or no advantages to the Japanese. Further, Western nations brought new clothing styles, manners, and customs that many traditional-minded Japanese came to resent.

In 1867, warriors from Choshu and Satsuma, two provinces in southern Japan, banded together and ousted the shogun. They then restored the emperor, Emperor Meiji at the time, as the head of

In May of 1932, soldiers of the Japanese Imperial Bodyguard gathered to present arms at the Yasukuni Shrine and honor the soldiers who had been killed in battle.

Japan. However, the real rulers of Japan were the samurai who had carried out this revolution. Their first goal was to strengthen Japan to fight off further Western influence and interference. The concept of *fukoku kyohei*—"rich country, strong army"—became the motto Japan would not just live by but thrive on.

Japan did learn one thing from its dealings with Western nations—the combination of militarism and imperialism made a nation powerful. If a nation had needs or desires, its military was a means to fulfill them. While Japan understood that diplomatic means were always ideal, it also knew that military power would win more disagreements than friendly words and pleasant smiles.

Japan's first venture into imperialism took place in Korea. Japanese ambassadors and gunboats convinced Korea to open its ports to trade with Japan. The Japanese were not content to stop there, however. They wanted to create a Japanese empire that encompassed all of Asia. The Japanese justified their newfound desire for domination by believing that by conquering the other nations of Asia, Japan would be saving these Asian nations from humiliation at the hands of Western nations.

The way of the warrior had now become the lifestyle of Japanese citizens. As children, the Japanese attended schools run with military efficiency. In school, the children did learn math, reading, and writing. They learned, too, about loyalty, devotion to the Japanese emperor, and patriotism for their country. As adults, men were expected to serve for three years in either the army or the navy, as well as another four years in the military reserves. The pride of Japan depended on a strong military. Many people joined patriotic societies such as the Gen'yosha (Black Ocean Society) or Kokuryukai (Black Dragon Society). These groups were prowar, promilitary, and pro-Japan. The Japanese people even believed that bringing about political change through assassination was not only acceptable but understandable as well. Assassination for patriotic purposes was considered a crime of passion and one that people received only light punishments for committing. The assassins, especially those belonging to the Japanese military, became heroes in the eyes of many Japanese people.

Militarism is the doctrine of a society in which military concepts and principles affect not only the politics and economy of a nation but also the everyday lives of its people. There was never a more militaristic culture than that of twentieth-century Japan. Patriotism and nationalism infused Japan with an almost intoxicating sense of power. It was this belief that led Japan to war—first on a regional scale, and eventually across the Pacific.

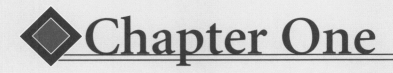

Chapter One

The Early Roots
of Militarism

Japan entered the twentieth century with a long history of political, military, and social traditions that affected its national development and worldview. Chief among these traditions were centuries of rule by shoguns, or military leaders, and the existence of a special class of warriors called samurai. These two traditions are considered largely responsible for establishing a military culture in the Japanese psyche.

Officially, Japan was governed by an emperor to whom people swore loyalty. Real power, however, lay in the hands of the shogun and his samurai. The shogun set tax rates, decided whether Japan would go to war, and oversaw the system of justice. The shogun determined where members of the aristocracy lived and what lifestyle the emperor would be allowed.

A succession of shoguns governed Japan for seven centuries, which firmly established a tradition of rule by military leaders. These leaders either minimized the emperor's political involvement or completely excluded the emperor from decision making. Thus, shoguns set the precedent for military leaders, not civilian leaders, to make national political and economic decisions.

Shoguns and Samurai

Beginning in the twelfth century, powerful landowners called *daimyo* began to hire professional warriors to protect their property. These warriors were called samurai, which means "in service" or "in the service of." Wealth and power were determined by how much land a person held. The daimyo needed samurai to protect their holdings from enemies who would try to seize the land, and therefore the power, of the daimyo. Samurai fought to expand their daimyo's property as well, which would increase the daimyo's

power. Over time, the daimyo's wealth and power were measured by not only the amount of land he owned but also by how many samurai he commanded.

Samurai enjoyed many of the same privileges as the daimyo, including higher social status and the ability to travel freely. Additionally, samurai were permitted to wear swords, one long and one short, at a time when others were not permitted to display weapons. The swords served as more than weapons. They defined a samurai's social status.

All daimyo and samurai answered to the shogun, the highest military commander. The term *shogun* translates literally as "commander in chief for the suppression of barbarians." The emperor awarded the title of shogun. In practice, however, the shogun wielded more power than the emperor did, whose role was primarily a figurehead. Over time, the title of shogun became permanent and hereditary, passed on within a single family.

A succession of shoguns ruled Japan for seven centuries, from 1185 to 1868. These seven centuries are divided into time periods known as shogunates. Each shogunate was assigned a name based on either the city from which the shogun governed or the family to which the shogun belonged.

The government of the shogun was called the *bakufu* and served as the central administration for all Japan. The bakufu was made up of the shogun and four or five close advisers. This council created national policy and supervised the daimyo and samurai.

When a shogun's power was challenged, the shogun ordered his most loyal daimyo to correct the situation. One such problem was tax collection. In an order written in 1186, a shogun openly stated his annoyance with rebel samurai who refused to pay their taxes:

> [F]orthwith others shall cease to commit outrages and obey the commands of the *ji-to* (administrator). … He shall give security to the people, and … administer the annual taxes. … [I]t is reported that *bushi* (warriors) … commit willful outrages, [preventing the collection of] the annual taxes, and yearly refusing [their own payments]. These are exceedingly wrongful acts.[1]

The First Shogunate

The first shoguns came from the Minamoto family, whose power was based in the city of Kamakura. Consequently, this time in Japanese history is referred to as either the Minamoto era or the Kamakura period.

In 1180, the Minamoto family took control of Japan by defeating a rival family in a civil war. Following this success, the emperor appointed the head of the family, Minamoto Yorimoto, as the first shogun. Minamoto's appointment marked the

Only high-ranking samurai warriors were permitted to fight on horseback.

Early samurai fought mostly with bow and arrow. Battles with the Mongols in the 1400s changed the weapon of choice to the samurai sword.

Minamoto Yoritomo (on horseback) acquired the title of supreme commander, or shogun, in 1192 and ruled until his death on February 9, 1199.

change from a regime governed by nobles to one governed by samurai.

Minamoto Yorimoto shared power with the emperor. His successors did not. They expanded the role of shogun to exclude the emperor from day-to-day governing of Japan.

The system that emerged resembled the feudal system that existed in Europe during this same time. Feudalism is a system of government based on the exchange of land for service or loyalty. In Japan, the shogun awarded the land, and

warriors owed allegiance to the shogun rather than to the emperor.

During the Kamakura period, samurai culture became more clearly defined. Samurai were expected to behave according to an unwritten code of behavior instilled in them during their training. This code, called Bushido, was based on Buddhist principles. Bushido did not tell samurai how to fight as much as it told them how to live. A samurai was expected to master the tools of a warrior, such as riding horses and using swords, as well

Losing Face

A samurai's behavior reflected on his family, his daimyo, his shogun, and his emperor. The worst crime a samurai could commit was to lose face, or do something dishonorable. Dishonorable acts included being taken prisoner in battle or being disloyal to a daimyo. To behave dishonorably was to disgrace the samurai and his family, daimyo, shogun, and emperor. A disgraced samurai was stripped of his swords, his rank, and his privileges. He was expelled from his family and his territory.

To save his honor, a samurai could commit suicide. This act of suicide, called *seppuku* or *hara kiri*, would redeem a samurai's honor only if he followed certain rules. For example, the samurai had to wear the proper white ceremonial clothing, perform an elaborate tea ceremony, and have a witness testify that he had followed all the prescribed seppuku rituals. Only if all the proper rituals were followed in front of a witness would a samurai regain his honor in death.

as the tools of the aristocracy, such as education and the arts. Thus, samurai were trained to be fierce, brutal warriors on the battlefield and refined, courteous gentlemen off it. According to Bushido, in peace and in war, a true samurai must demonstrate the qualities of courage, loyalty, truthfulness, compassion, and above all else, honor. As historian W. G. Beasley describes,

> The [Minamoto military] campaigns and the stories they engendered had a vital place in shaping the warrior code. Courage and loyalty had remained its central themes, as they had always been. Taking part in set-piece battles … provided a wider audience for the incidents in which these qualities were displayed. In

such a situation, warriors became more aware of the good opinion of their fellows. Loyalty, a manly sentiment, began to take precedence over other, less urgent ties, like duty to wives and family.[2]

Women could not become samurai. The mothers, wives, and daughters of samurai, however, were expected to be as brave, loyal, and honorable as their warrior relatives were. Consequently, the samurai code and its emphasis on honor became deeply embedded in Japanese culture.

The Second Shogunate

The emperor appointed Ashikaga Takauji as shogun in 1338, and the bakufu was moved to Muromachi. This marked the beginning of the Ashikaga era and Muromachi period. This shogunate was marked by the increased power of the daimyo. They fought each other for military supremacy by attacking neighbors and seizing their land.

Within ten years, the bakufu was torn apart by civil war. The followers of Ashikaga were forced to side with either the shogun, Takauji, or his brother Tadayoshi. Takauji's son, Tadafuyu, held an official position as deputy in Nagato. When Tadafuyu lost his post to his uncle's forces, Tadafuyu called for men to join him in the military. In 1350, he sent out a summons: "In order to rest the minds of the two lords, [Tadafuyu] has started [his military enterprise]. It is hereby commanded that you shall speedily hasten to his side and render loyal service."[3] In the Ashikaga era, such a summons was not a request but a demand. Tadafuyu had to prove his loyalty to his father, Ashikaga Takauji, by retaking any land or property lost during the rebellion.

Later in the Ashikaga era, a few daimyo began to restore order and reunify the country. As they did so, they acquired great wealth. They spent this wealth by building elaborate castles and Buddhist temples. Their efforts were not enough to keep the country at peace.

The Ashikaga era was followed by nearly a century of civil war that ended with a battle at Sekigahara. The winner was Tokugawa Ieyasu, leader of the Tokugawa family. The shogunate he established was the longest and most peaceful in Japan's history.

The Tokugawa Era

The Tokugawa ruled from the city of Edo, known today as Tokyo. To maintain order and control, the Tokugawa made harsh laws and placed severe restrictions on both social and geographic mobility. Individuals had no rights under the Tokugawa regime. The population lived under a strict class system, which required all people to show respect for everyone in levels above them.

The Tokugawa held especially tight control over the daimyo. The shogun restricted their activities and dictated where the daimyo lived. Daimyo deemed the most loyal lived closest to the shogun. Those considered least loyal were given lands far away from the capital. The shogun required the daimyo to build a second home at Edo and insisted that the daimyo's wives and children stay there. Each daimyo spent six months of the year at the shogun's castle in Edo. When daimyo returned to their own estates, their wives and children became the shogun's hostages. Such hostage keeping guaranteed that the daimyo would return to Edo and remain loyal to the shogun. This system of travel and hostage keeping is called the *sankin-kotai* system. Sankin-kotai was the shogun's way of preventing rebellion. A daimyo who was constantly traveling did not have the time or resources to rebel.

The Social Pyramid

Tokugawa Japan had a rigid system of social ranking. People rarely left the class into which they and their parents had been born. Each class served the classes above it.

The shogun and emperor held the highest positions. They were served by daimyo, who were awarded estates by the shogun based on demonstrated loyalty to the shogun.

Each daimyo had an army of samurai. In exchange for a samurai's military service, he was given a number of farmers to oversee. The samurai's wealth was based on the amount of rice he could collect from those farmers.

Artisans and peasants were next on the social pyramid, but they were not at the lowest level. The lowest members of Japanese society were the merchants, who were considered dirty because their livelihoods depended on money.

In Tokugawa society, each class served the class above it.

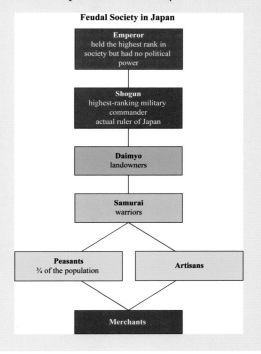

Feudal Society in Japan

Emperor
held the highest rank in society but had no political power

Shogun
highest-ranking military commander
actual ruler of Japan

Daimyo
landowners

Samurai
warriors

Peasants
¾ of the population

Artisans

Merchants

The Tokugawa expelled most foreigners from Japan. The only foreigners allowed to remain were the Dutch, who were confined to a small compound near the city of Nagasaki. Shoguns sought to remove the influence of Christianity, which they perceived as a tool of economic control used by foreigners. Expelling foreigners prevented the daimyo from gaining power through trade with outsiders.

Expelling foreigners resulted in an additional, unforeseen consequence. Dur-

Osaka Castle was originally built by Hideyoshi Toyotomi, the chief imperial minister of Japan, in 1583. It was destroyed and later rebuilt by the Tokugawa shoguns in the 1600s.

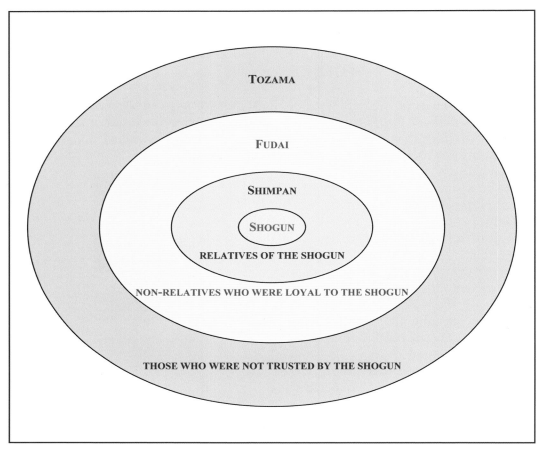

The deployment of the daimyo helped maintain peace and prevent rebellions during the Tokugawa or Edo Era (1603–1868).

ing Japan's period of self-imposed isolation, the Industrial Revolution occ-urred in the West. Scientific, technological, and military advancements of the industrial era bypassed the remote and isolated Japan.

A Time of Relative Peace

The Tokugawa era is perhaps best kno-wn for the absence of warfare. This re-sulted from the balance of power that the shoguns established through their many controls. The peaceful Tokugawa era left samurai without income, how-ever. As a result, samurai lost power and much of the land they had controlled. To remedy the situation, the government sought to keep the samurai busy and distracted. The bakufu emphasized the importance of education and culture, claiming that being educated and cultured brought honor to a samurai and his family. Many samurai studied art and philosophy and became civil servants, teachers of martial arts, scholars, writers, or poets.

Samurai who had contact with the Dutch settlement at Nagasaki acquired education and culture that the Tokugawa did not anticipate. Through Dutch traders, these samurai learned of Western advancements and ideas. This information allowed them to see how far behind the rest of the world Japan was falling.

The backwardness of their country offended the samurai's sense of honor. They began to plot ways to recapture the glory they felt was due Japan. While the shoguns worked to keep daimyo loyal, they did not see the rebellion

Today, a Dutch town is recreated at the Huis Ten Bosch theme park in Nagaski. The park features replicas of Dutch houses, windmills, and a royal residence.

growing among the samurai. When Japan's isolation from the world ended, the subsequent explosion by the samurai caused the downfall of the Tokugawa shogunate.

The Opening of Japan to Foreign Trade

At various times during the late eighteenth century, ships from the United States, Russia, and Britain began to call at Japanese ports, seeking to open trade between Japan and the West. These explorers had heard tales of Japan's wealth, and they wanted a piece of it for their countries. Reaction to the visitors was mixed.

The Tokugawa wanted nothing to do with foreigners. They saw no need to change a system that kept themselves in power. To some extent, opponents of trade with the West feared what international trade and the end of isolation would mean for the existing social structure. Opening Japan to trade meant opening opportunities for Japan's merchants to gain wealth and power. The Tokugawa's carefully crafted social pyramid would collapse.

Some Japanese encouraged contact with the West. Word had leaked into Japan that Western countries had all but carved up China into a series of colonies. China had been too weak, politically and militarily, to resist. A number of samurai feared Japan would meet the same fate. To them, Japan's best recourse was fukoku kyohei, which means "enrich the country, strengthen the military." Officials, such as Sakuma Shozan, began pressuring the bakufu to acquire technology that might be used to defend Japan, arguing that "Japan must prepare for attack, both by purchasing modern armaments and by learning to make them, too."[4] Achieving those goals meant contact and selective trade with the West. Sakuma advocated the policy he called "Eastern ethics, Western science." According to this policy, Japan would acquire and use Western technology without giving up traditional Japanese values and culture.

In 1853, U.S. naval commodore Matthew Perry anchored four gunboats, called black ships by the Japanese, in Tokyo Bay. He had been sent by President Millard Fillmore to force Japan to accept trade with the United States. In a letter dated November 13, 1852, Fillmore wrote, "I am desirous that our two countries should trade with each other, for the benefit both of Japan and the United States."[5]

Despite the friendly tone of Fillmore's letter, Perry's warships were meant as a show of force to intimidate the Tokugawa into accepting U.S. trade terms. The United States wanted assurances that Japan would provide food, goods, and fuel to ships arriving in Japan.

Japan tried to hold off giving the United States its decision. It took a year to produce a response, in part because the emperor had died and a new emperor had taken his place. Further, the general attitude of the Japanese toward change was negative. They did not wish to abandon old laws and old traditions in favor of developing questionable relationships with foreign nations.

When the government finally responded to Fillmore and Perry, the letter said, "[W]e admit the urgency, and shall entirely comply with the proposals of your government concerning coal, wood, water, provisions, and the saving of ships and their crews in distress. After being informed which harbor your excellency selects, that harbor shall be prepared, which preparation is estimated will take five years."[6]

Fearing they were no longer able to maintain their isolationist policy on foreign trade, Japanese leaders entered into the Kanagawa Treaty of Friendship in 1854. The treaty opened the ports of Shimoda and Hakodate to U.S. ships.

Treaties with other Western nations followed.

Because of Japan's centuries of isolation, its leaders were ill equipped for the foreign negotiations that created these treaties. They did not know what to ask for or how to haggle over terms. Consequently, foreign powers usually walked away from treaty talks with everything they wanted. Such one-sided agreements showcased the growing weakness of the bakufu and further offended the honor of the increasingly discontented samurai.

Japanese ultranationalists continued to oppose opening Japan to the outside world. They considered Japan sacred and the presence of foreigners on Japanese soil as pollution. These ultranationalists became known as Shishi soldiers. They

Ultranationalism

Nationalism is a belief in the importance and superiority of an individual's country or ethnic group. It has often been used as a tool to gain popular support for military action. Japanese nationalism is thought to have flourished in response to the West's poor treatment of Japan from Matthew Perry's first contact in 1853.

Ultranationalism is an extreme form of nationalism, identified most often with Germany, Italy, and Japan in the 1920s and 1930s. Japan's resentment of its treatment by the West after World War I led to the development of an ultranationalist ideology that glorified Japan and claimed superiority over the West. This ideology was used to justify military growth and the pursuit of military solutions to Japan's problems. Ultranationalism, fed by resentment of the West and difficult economic conditions during the Great Depression, inspired overwhelming support for Japanese conquest and expansion through military means, a familiar theme throughout Japan's history.

were known for being die-hard and hot-blooded, willing to sacrifice their lives to further the cause of patriotism. The Shishi rallied behind the slogan *sonno-joi*, which means "honor the emperor, expel the barbarian." For them, the shogun had betrayed Japan by signing treaties with the foreigners. They felt that the only way for Japan to regain its honor was to take negotiating power away from the shogun and give it to the emperor. A period of violence followed the signing of the commercial treaties. Eventually, there was grudging acceptance. The Japanese realized that they could not prevent the fleets from arriving and they did not have the military power to fight off foreign fleets.

Nonetheless, the seeds of rebellion had been planted. Samurai discontent, coupled with exposure to Western ideas and technology, brought an end to the Tokugawa shogunate. Historian W. G. Beasley explains:

Many saw the foreign threat as a problem which could only be solved by making significant political changes within Japan, or by adopting methods, such as the use of Western military science and industrial technology, which would have profound implications for the nature of Japanese culture and society.[7]

The peace and stability of the Tokugawa era had ended. While the shogunate was reaching its conclusion, however, the rule of military leaders was not. The tradition of military leaders governing civilian populations continued. Centuries of shogunate rule had embedded in the Japanese psyche the belief that military force was a legitimate means for achieving its goals: to protect itself from outside threats and demonstrate the greatness of Japan.

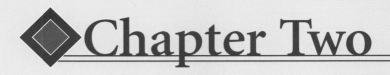

Chapter Two

The Meiji Restoration

Under Tokugawa rule, Japan had been at peace. The Tokugawa had ruled with an iron fist for more than two centuries. By the late nineteenth century, their leadership had led to a failing economy, high rates of taxation, and serious food shortages. Some samurai grew concerned. The arrival of U.S. naval forces and the opening of Japan to foreign trade was the last straw. The samurai saw foreigners taking advantage of Japanese rulers and they felt their nation had become too weak to fight back.

The samurai's solution was a *coup d'etat*, the sudden overthrowing of the current government resulting in the seizure of political power. The samurai's coup d'etat was a surprisingly quick and easy revolt. Although the samurai were an elite, privileged class in Japan, they still sought change in their nation's government. This was because the samurai were not allowed to own land or exercise any real power, even though they were part of the upper class. For centuries, they had been little more than a group of elite, upper-class employees.

Revolution and Change

A group of rebellious samurai from Satsuma and Choshu, two provinces in southern Japan, overthrew Japan's government in 1868. The samurai's goals were clear: strengthen Japan's military and economy, end Japan's crumbling political order, and create a society in which talented, intelligent people, regardless of their background, could advance. By achieving these goals, the samurai felt Japan's national pride would be restored, and Japan could become a world power.

One of the samurai's first actions as a result of the revolution was to restore an emperor as the head of Japan's government. They chose Prince Mutsuhito to become Japan's new emperor. Mutsuhi-to became the 122nd emperor of Japan. He took the name *Meiji*, which means "enlightened rule." Though Meiji was now the emperor, he was merely a figure-head. The true power sat in the hands of a select group of men who had taken part in the revolution. Despite the restoration of the emperor, the nation was actually governed by an oligarchy, or a form of government in which the ruling power belongs to a small group of people. Emperor Meiji merely dressed in fancy uniforms and became a dominant symbol of Japan for the nation's people.

The oligarchy did write a charter when they established the new government. The Charter Oath of 1868 set forth the principles for their vision of Japan's future. The first three articles of the oath allowed citizens to pursue jobs of their own choosing, attend political meetings, and participate in the government. The oath also stated that "Evil customs of the past shall be broken off and everything based upon the just laws of Nature. Knowledge shall be sought throughout the world so as to strengthen the foundations of imperial rule."[8] This was radical thinking for the Japanese people. After centuries of jobs gained solely by inheritance, people could now achieve their own success using their own skills and talents. Equally important, the Japanese government agreed to study what they felt were the most superior aspects of Western culture and then introduce them into Japanese government, education, and business practices.

It was important to its leaders that the new government of Japan be seen as something completely different from the old regime. To demonstrate that a new era in Japanese government had dawned, the emperor and his court were moved from Kyoto to Edo. Edo was renamed Tokyo and officially declared Japan's capital city.

Emperor Meiji became the idol of the Japanese people. As a poet, he produced about one hundred thousand poems known as *waka* poetry. In addition to their merit as literary works, these poems fostered significant teachings to intensify nationalism and Japan's moral character. This can be seen in the following poem, written by Emperor Meiji:

> For the times to come
> And of meeting what must be met
> All of our people
> Must be taught to walk along
> The path of sincerity[9]

The Power Behind the Emperor

One of the first acts of the Meiji oligarchy was to unify the nation under a central government. To do this, it was necessary to get rid of the daimyo's domains and the shogun system that had been in power for over six hundred years. The government leaders asked the daimyo to

Prince Matsuhito was only 15 when he ascended the Emperor's throne in 1867.

Shinto

Under Meiji rule, Shinto became the state religion of Japan. The emperor was the head of the Shinto religion. The name *Shinto* comes from two Chinese characters, *shin* and *tao*. They combine to mean "way of the spirits." The basic element of Shinto is devotion to spiritual beings and forces of nature. The practice of Shinto enables people to communicate with these spiritual beings, which are called *kami*.

The Shinto religion views people as essentially good. Followers believe that all experiences in life are connected to this world and that there is no afterlife. There is no division between the natural and supernatural world. Everything connects to a single, unified universe. Followers of Shinto participate in festivals and attend shrines in their local areas. Shrine visitors write their wishes on wooden plates and leave them on an *ema* (display board). Typical wishes include good health, happiness, wealth, success in business, or a passing grade on a test.

voluntarily give up their domains to the emperor. In 1871, the political organization of Japan changed from 180 domains to 72 prefectures. Prefectures are regional districts of Japan managed by a governor. Many former daimyo became governors of lands that they had once owned and ruled.

The group that put Emperor Meiji on the throne established the Council of State as the highest political power in Japan. This council consisted of prominent samurai leaders that had been part of the revolution. The council was revised in 1869 and then replaced in 1871 by three powerful groups: the Center, the Left, and the Right. Individual government departments managed the offices of public works, finance, and foreign affairs,

among others. Japan's government even established an Office of Shinto Worship that became more important than the Council of State.

Under the shogunates, land ownership had been based on inheritance. The new government wanted to redistribute the land in a more democratic way. Under the new land-tax system, the Japanese government considered the landowner to be the person who paid taxes on that land. Under the old system, taxes could be paid in rice or other crops. From 1873 onward, taxes had to be paid in money. The standard tax rate became 3 percent of the assessed land value. Later laws reduced the tax rate to even less. As part of the redistribution of land, the Japanese government had to arrange a nationwide land assessment program to find out how much each plot was worth.

The Power of the Military

Once the restoration of Japan was underway, government leaders turned their attention to building a stronger military. Under the shogunates, each daimyo had a personal army of samurai who were armed with traditional Japanese weapons. The new military would be national in scope, reporting—on the surface—to Japan's emperor. The true powers behind the military, though, were three leaders from the Choshu province: Kido Koin, Omura Masujiro, and Yamagata Aritomo. These men decided that the Japanese military needed to be improved from the bottom up. They hoped to develop a world-class army and navy similar to those of Western nations.

Their military reorganization began with setting up national arsenals for weapons and military training schools. Yamagata used his own experience as a military commander as well as in-depth studies of the French army for the foundation of the new Japanese army. The start-up army began with nine thousand imperial guards whose job was to protect Japan from within the four regional garrisons, or army posts, that the new government had established. Yamagata became the first commander of these imperial guards.

The new Japanese navy required modern military vessels armed with modern military weapons. While Japan did have a long seagoing history, Japanese ships of the past had been designed primarily for fishing and trading. For now, the few remaining shogunate vessels would have to form the core of Japan's new navy, but these few ships were not enough to create a truly world-class navy. Japan would need to work to improve its navy.

In 1873, Yamagata introduced an idea for developing a larger, more productive military: conscription, or draft. This plan broke with all prior Japanese military traditions. No longer would the army be dependent on samurai alone, but rather on Japan's entire male population. This opened the door for able-bodied men of all classes to become part of Japan's growing military force. All twenty-year-old Japanese males, regardless of their social status, were eligible for the draft. Those who were drafted served three years as active duty soldiers or sailors in the army or navy, as well as an additional four years in the reserves. Through this system, Japan would be able to call upon fully trained, fully committed men to fill the ranks of their army and navy in the event of a war.

The Japanese citizens, however, did not take well to this draft, partially because the conscription law had too many exemptions. Men who were the heads of a household, criminals, students, teachers, or deemed physically unfit did not have to serve in Japan's military. Further adding to the outrage was the fact that the wealthy could buy their way out of military service for 270 yen, which was "more than the annual wage of a common laborer. Large numbers of people sought to qualify for exemption or somehow scrape together the buyout fee. The army had trouble meeting the quotas for what the government itself labeled a 'blood tax.'"[10]

The People's Rights

It was expected that military training would produce the type of citizens the new government wanted. The government believed Japanese men returning from military service would embody the true sense of nationalism and display the discipline essential to creating a richer, stronger Japan. What was not expected, though, was the public's reaction to the draft. Riots broke out in sixteen military recruitment centers. The rioters destroyed property and created chaos in the streets of Japan. The government stepped in quickly and punished more than one hundred thousand of these protestors for their involvement in the riots.

After failing with the adult population, Japanese officials then determined that the next route to nationalism ran through its children. During the Meiji Restoration, education became required. School combined academic subjects such as reading, writing, mathematics, and history with practical skills and patriotism. As with other government departments, the Ministry of Education modeled its schools on the Western system.

Japanese students were taught to follow laws and obey their parents. Schools displayed portraits of the emperor in every classroom. Students repeated the Imperial Rescript of Education much like American students say the Pledge of Allegiance. The Imperial Rescript of Education's text included set patterns of behavior expected of all students:

Ye, Our subjects, be filial to your parents, affectionate to your brothers and sisters; as husbands and wives be harmonious, as friends true; bear yourselves in modesty and moderation; extend your benevolence to all; pursue learning and cultivate arts, and thereby develop intellectual faculties and perfect moral powers; furthermore advance public good and promote common interests; always respect the Japanese Constitution and observe the laws; should emergency arise, offer yourselves courageously to the State; and thus guard and maintain the prosperity of Our Imperial Throne coeval [contemporary] with heaven and earth.[11]

Even teachers were expected to follow the almost military structure of schooling. Teacher training schools required military uniforms and strict, military-style discipline. Thus, Japanese schools became factories that manufactured patriots.

In Japan's schools, the authority of teachers and the government went unquestioned. In cities, towns, and villages, however, this was not the case. Citizens resented mandatory education, high taxes, and what they considered a lack of personal freedoms. The Japanese people protested in favor of earning popular rights. In the mid-1870s, the protestors found a leader among the old guard: Saigo Takamori.

After the Meiji Restoration, Saigo had retreated to a remote village of Kagoshima in Satsuma. There, Saigo lived the life of a samurai. He became leader of the citizens of Kagoshima when they refused to pay taxes or follow many of the new laws instituted by the Meiji government. Their protest expanded into military action. In 1877, Saigo led fourteen thousand soldiers in the Satsuma Rebellion. As they marched to confront the Imperial Japanese Army, more and more Japanese joined Saigo and his troops. Eventually, Saigo had more than forty thousand troops under his command.

The Satsuma Rebellion was doomed to fail. The Imperial Japanese Army, as new as it was, was still better armed. It had been trained in Western military techniques. The Imperial Japanese Army's defeat of Saigo and his rebel troops produced two results. First, it ended any ideas of rebellion by other samurai and unhappy citizens. Second, it established the Imperial Japanese Army as a competent, successful military unit—exactly what the Japanese government had hoped to produce.

Industrialization

For Japan to become a world power, it needed not just a modern military, but a strong economy as well. As Japanese officials toured Western nations, they investigated business and manufacturing plants. The Industrial Revolution that

The Last Samurai

Soldier and statesman Saigo Takamori (1828–1877) represented the end of an era in Japanese culture. Saigo belonged to the group of Satsuma samurai who had once supported the Meiji Restoration.

Saigo believed in the samurai code of behavior and felt that the new government had forgotten the value of honor. When his proposal for invading Korea was rejected by the government, Saigo retreated to an outpost in Kagoshima. There, he founded a military school that attracted many disheartened followers of the samurai tradition.

The Satsuma, or Samurai, Rebellion began in 1877. After three weeks of fighting, Saigo's troops had suffered twenty thousand casualties and their defeat was clear. Saigo acknowledged their loss. To save his honor, he decided to commit seppuku. Saigo died on September 24, 1877. He is often considered the last real samurai.

had swept across Europe and North America in the earlier part of the century had finally reached Japan.

In 1880, three out of four Japanese workers labored on farms. Agriculture produced four-fifths of Japan's tax revenue. Now industrialization brought changes to Japan in much the same way it had changed European countries. The population of Japan, like the populations of Europe and the United States, shifted from a farm-based, rural population to an industrial-based, urban population.

One of the first industries to become successful in Japan was the textile industry. In 1882, Shibusawa Eiichi opened the Osaka Spinning Company. Shibusawa employed steam power to run his mill— a concept that became popular in many Japanese textile mills. This modern textile factory became the model for other textile mills that produced quality silk and cotton.

The Japanese textile industry, unfortunately, grew through the labor of poor young women. Many girls saw the opportunity to leave the family farm and work in the city as glamorous, but they were wrong. Women working in textile factories did receive free lodging, but their quarters were overcrowded dormitories run almost like prisons. The food provided by their employers was often inedible. Plus, workers endured twelve-hour shifts with few breaks and poor wages. Punishments for labor problems were also severe. Said one worker interviewed by a government official, "If anyone steals something, she is stripped naked and

marched around the factory with a flag attached to her shoulders. They then take her to the dining hall and report her misdeed to everybody."[12] Factory owners ignored simple rights of workers, looking only toward their profits.

Once industrialization in Japan began, change came quickly. From 1890 to 1900, manufacturing in Japan doubled. It doubled again between 1900 and 1914. Japanese mines churned out coal and iron ore. Foundries smelted metal into steel. Raw materials and finished goods sped along private and government railroad lines that connected the Japanese cities of Hokkaido, Yokohama, Nagoya, Kyoto, and Hiroshima. In addition to household goods, the Japanese developed a thriving munitions industry, building cannons, weapons, ammunition, and ships for the military. The concept of fukoku kyohei —rich country, strong army—was coming true.

The Meiji Constitution

By the late 1800s, everything the rebels had fought for and planned had come to fruition. The new government had built a rich country and a strong army— fukoku kyohei. Now it was time for Japan to formalize its achievements in a constitution. The document would be presented as a gift from Emperor Meiji to the Japanese citizens. It took a year and a half to finish the document, which was finally presented on February 11, 1889.

Unlike the United States Constitution, which had to be approved by all states

By the early 1920s, women factory workers were actively protesting the low wages and poor working conditions they were forced to endure.

before it could go into effect, the Meiji Constitution was reviewed and approved by only the inner circle of power—the twelve members of the oligarchy—the emperor's privy council.

The constitution set forth the concept that the people and the emperor should rule Japan together. On the surface, the emperor could appoint officials, create laws, call together a national legislature, reorganize the departments and ministries of the government, make treaties, and declare both war and peace. In reality, the oligarchy had no intention of the

Political Slogans

When citizens from the provinces of Satsuma and Choshu rebelled against the Tokugawa shogunate, their battle cry had been "*Sonno joi*," or "Honor the emperor, expel the barbarians." Because the United States and Europe had both made trade arrangements with Japan that had benefited only the Western nations, Japan felt it had been humiliated. The Imperial Court had also wanted to oust foreign influence from Japan, but it had been powerless to do so. Ultimately, the Japanese people believed that they had lost face in the international community.

Japan knew it could not win against American or European military power, nor could Japan force these Western nations to renegotiate deals that were unfavorable to Japan. Nonetheless, Japanese provinces continued to trade with Western nations, building up Japan's store of artillery, ships, ammunition, and other military needs. During the Meiji Restoration, the slogan changed from *sonno joi* to *fukoku kyohei*—rich country, strong army.

emperor exercising such powers. Any actions or decrees from the emperor had to be approved by the emperor's privy council.

According to Ito Hirobumi, an author of the Meiji Constitution,

The spirit behind the establishment of constitutional government is first to impose restrictions on the powers of the monarch, and second to secure the rights of subjects. … In whatever country, when you do not protect the rights of subjects and do not limit the power of the monarch, you have a despotic government, in which the rights of the ruler have become as unlimited as the duties of the subjects.[13]

The constitution called for the establishment of a legislative body, called a diet. The Imperial Diet first met in 1890 with both a House of Representatives and a House of Peers. Voting was limited to adult males only, who then chose representatives. The House of Peers consisted of noblemen. For any law to go into effect, that law had to be approved by both the Diet and the emperor. According to the Meiji Constitution, the head of the Japanese government was now the prime minister, an official chosen by the emperor.

The changes that occurred in Japan during the Meiji Restoration came about because Japan did not want foreign interference. Ironically, Japan planned to use the same ideas learned from the West

The Hierarchy of the Japanese Government in the Meiji Period

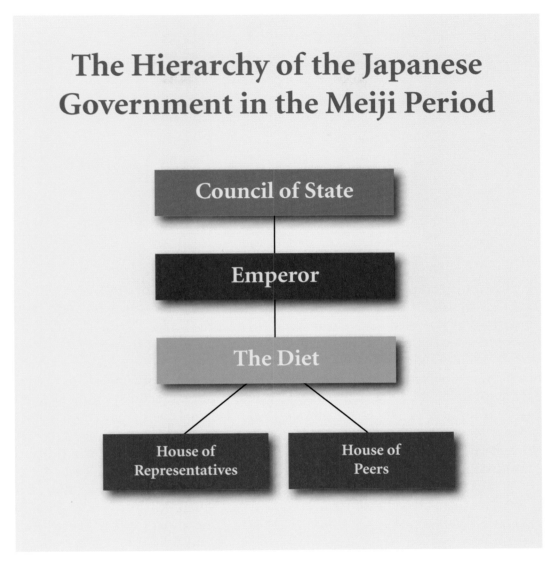

The Meiji Constitution ensured a balance of power. Each branch of government had to cooperate with the others in order to achieve its goals.

in order to block further Western influence. It built its strong army and rich country using Western ideas. To achieve world-power status, Japanese leaders did what Western nations had done before them—they looked elsewhere to expand Japan's influence. Mainland Asia and the nations of Korea and China became the first targets of the newly powerful Japan.

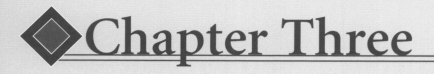

Chapter Three

Times of Trouble

Japan learned an important lesson from its dealings with Western nations: if you need land, a seaport, or workers—take them. Great Britain, with its colonies and territories throughout the world, served as an ideal model. France, Germany, and the United States had acquired major holdings in Asia too.

Japanese imperialism began with the arrival of U.S. naval commodore Matthew Perry in a Japanese harbor in 1853. The United States wanted to become trading partners with Japan and achieved its goal using threats and intimidation against Japan. It was not long before Japan began to use the same tactics themselves. In 1875, Japan followed the United States' example and forced Korea to open the ports of Pusan, Wonsan, and Inchon to Japanese trade. The Treaty of Gangwha humiliated the Koreans in the same way that treaties with Western nations had humiliated the Japanese. Japan, the self-anointed victim of Western bullying, had now become the bully.

Koreans did not look kindly on Japan's interference in their country. According to historian Peter Duus, "many Korean scholars and officials regarded the Japanese as 'Oriental renegades' who had betrayed their heritage by shamelessly imitating the Western countries."[14] In 1882, the Japanese sent advisers to watch out for Japan's interests in Korea. Korean soldiers, angry because of unpaid wages, killed their Japanese military adviser, set fire to the Japanese government offices, and threatened the Japanese minister. China, seeing this as an opportunity to push itself farther into Korea, sent five thousand troops to support the rebel soldiers. The joint effort forced Japan to leave Korea, and now Chinese officials and advisers replaced the ones from Japan.

In 1894, Japan and China went to war over Korea. At first, it seemed unlikely that Japan would win the Sino-Japanese War. China's army far outnumbered Japan's, and the Chinese navy had twice as many warships as the Japanese navy did. Japan was not concerned. The Japanese proved that training combined with strategy was more important than simply having the larger military. First, Japan took control of the Yellow Sea, a large inlet of the Pacific Ocean lying between China and Korea. Then, Japanese troops landed in Korea and established control over the Liaodong Peninsula in Manchuria. Finally, during the bitter winter of 1895, Japan pushed farther into Manchuria and established positions overlooking ports that supplied the Chinese city of Beijing. The Chinese were forced to surrender.

When the war ended in 1895, the Chinese signed the Treaty of Shimonoseki. In the treaty, China acknowledged Korea's independence and gave Taiwan, the Pescadores Islands, and the Liaodong Peninsula in Manchuria to Japan. The Japanese forced China to pay 364 million

In 1894, during the first Sino-Japanese War, Japan celebrated one victorious battle by building a Triumphal Arch near Seoul, Korea.

During the Russo-Japanese war of 1904–1905, captured Russian warships were brought into Sasebo harbor flying Japanese flags.

yen to compensate Japan for its expenses from the war. This sum gave Japan a 50 percent profit on the war. More important, Japan had gained a solid presence in Korea. With its eyes on expansion, Japan never looked back.

The Taisho Era

As the twentieth century opened, Japan had achieved many of the goals set by the Meiji Restoration. Japan had built a central government, written a constitution, and founded an elected parliament. The nation could look back at rapid, successful industrialization, including an extensive railroad system that linked its rural and urban regions. Japan had gone from being a feudal state to becoming a modern, well-educated nation. The military boasted an army and navy equal to those of Western nations. Thus, and most important, the concept of fukoku kyohei—rich country, strong army—had been achieved.

In 1898, Japan and Russia signed an agreement that established Korea as a joint territory of both nations. A year later, rebellion broke out in China, and Russia sent troops to Manchuria to safeguard its interests in the region. The rebellion ended, but Russian troops did not leave Manchuria. Japan became concerned for its business interests in Manchuria and Korea. Japanese leaders took an unusual approach to this problem: they formed an alliance with Great Britain. Russia realized that a war with Japan now meant a war with Great Britain too.

By 1905, the situation between Japan and Russia over Manchuria and Korea reached a boiling point. Although Japan had easily defeated China in 1895, Russia was a far more challenging opponent. Japan engaged Russia in the Russo-Japanese War, but the war efforts did not go smoothly. Despite its alliance with Japan, Great Britain did not get involved, which improved Russia's chances for success.

Japan won an initial battle on the Liaodong Peninsula in Manchuria but later suffered serious losses elsewhere. Russia seemed on the verge of victory. Then the Japanese navy unexpectedly defeated the Russian fleet in a naval battle. After months of fighting and no clear winner, both sides wanted the conflict to end. Peace talks led to a treaty.

The Japanese people were displeased by the treaty conditions, which did not include any payments from Russia for war damages and did require that Japan and Russia share the Southern Manchuria Railroad. Riots broke out in major Japanese cities. Property was destroyed, pro-peace newspaper offices were attacked, and police arrested three hundred eleven people. Seventeen people died.

The Japanese people's inclination to riot did not end with the war. In 1906, two separate riots protesting increased streetcar fares erupted six months apart. Rioters smashed streetcars and attacked the streetcar companies' offices. Two years later, Tokyo citizens again rioted, this time against tax increases.

Regardless of the turmoil at home, Japan finally decided to make their hold over Korea official. In August 1910, Japan annexed Korea as a colony. Korea's prime minister Lee Wan-Yong signed the Japan-Korea Annexation Treaty, though he did not sign the document willingly. Once Korea signed the treaty, the Japanese immediately began to replace Korea's

Japan and Territories, 1894–1910

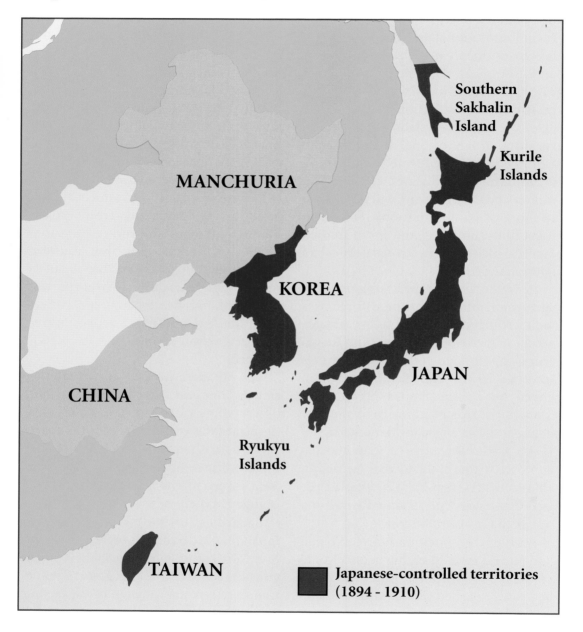

Between 1894 and 1910, Japan seized three major foreign territories—Taiwan, Korea and the Liaodong Peninsula in Southern Manchuria.

cultural heritage with Japanese customs and traditions. Public monuments were changed. Songs that were once sung to honor the Korean emperor were now sung in honor of the Japanese emperor.

In 1912, Emperor Meiji died. His son Yoshihito became the new emperor. Yoshihito chose to call his reign *Taisho*, meaning "great enlightenment." The Taisho emperor suffered from poor health. Many people close to him believed him to be mentally ill. As an infant, he had contracted meningitis, a disease that affects the central nervous system. It affected him for the rest of his life.

The emperor's obvious weakness and the aging of the Meiji leaders opened the government to new leadership. The Diet and political parties became stronger. Nationalism reached an extraordinary level. Japan believed its destiny was to protect and rule all of East Asia. Among the many goals Japan listed in its quest for dominance was the ousting of Western powers from Asia.

World War I

World War I came at the ideal moment for Japan. Japan wanted to reduce Western influences in Asia, and it would begin with attempting to oust Germany from Asia. In 1898, Germany had leased land and built a port in the Chinese city of Tsingtao. By early August 1914, Europe was engaged in World War I. Japan demanded that Germany "withdraw immediately from Japanese and Chinese waters the German men-o'-war and armed vessels of all kinds,

and to disarm at once those which cannot be withdrawn."[15]

Prepared to take the German port in Tsingtao by any means necessary, Japan readied its army for a siege against the Germans. Japan ultimately did declare war on Germany and its ally, Austria-Hungary, on August 25, 1914. Twenty-three thousand troops and one hundred forty-two guns began the siege on September 2, 1914. The siege lasted two months before the Germans finally surrendered on November 7, and Japan took possession of the port.

Japan's participation in World War I was minimal, but the war's impact on Japan was great. In January 1915, Japan presented China with the Twenty-one Demands. Within a few months, five more demands were added. The demands were meant to give Japan military, economic, and political influence in China. China was forced to agree with Japan's demands because, at the time, it did not have the strength to do otherwise.

By the time World War I ended, Japan had achieved many of its goals in Asia. It had secured its influence in China. The powers of Great Britain, France, and the United States officially recognized Japan's rights over Japan's newly held territories. Japan's economy had grown strong, too, as the nation increased its exports to its allies. Once again, Japan earned a profit from war.

One Crisis After Another

World War I devastated much of Europe,

Japanese soldiers flew their flag over a wrecked German gun machine after capturing the port of Tsingtao in 1914. More than 1,500 British troops assisted in the victory.

but it brought a wartime boom to Japan. The war had severed European traders' ties to Asian customers. This greatly helped Japan's new industrial economy by opening new markets for Japanese companies. Japanese factories worked at full capacity. Because so many men were involved in the military during the war,

people to work in these factories were in short supply. This allowed workers to demand higher salaries. Increased wages meant increased costs of many products. Even the prices of household goods increased rapidly in Japan at this time.

This brief period of plenty gave way to times of hardship in Japan. The price of

The Twenty-one Demands

On January 18, 1915, the Japanese government issued a list of twenty-one demands to the Chinese government. These demands were an attempt by Japan to gain influence with and authority over its neighbor. Japan gave China a choice: agree to their demands or expect war.

Japan's demands included the right to invest and build factories in Manchuria and Inner Mongolia. The Japanese demanded control of China's Shandong Peninsula as well. Other demands included the employment of Japanese citizens by China's government and the right of Japan to participate in China's negotiations with other countries. Additionally, China was told it had to buy at least half of its weapons and ammunition from Japanese companies.

The Chinese government agreed to all of Japan's demands. China had no other choice. However, the Chinese legislature never ratified the agreement, and after World War I ended, China refused to honor the Twenty-one Demands.

rice, for example, increased 174 percent between 1914 and 1920. Said one struggling teacher,

[M]y monthly income after deductions… is 18 yen and change…. There's no choice but to cut our rice costs a little by mixing in barley… and once a day making a meal of barley-rice gruel. Because charcoal is expensive, no one in the family has taken a bath for over a month, and we can hardly afford…a few pieces of meat, or even a single potato. [16]

In 1918, rice riots broke out in several of Japan's major cities. Rioters burned many corporate offices and other buildings. Shocked by the violence, political leaders called for a change. Japan's prime minister Terauchi Masaki was forced to resign. A period of tentative peace then came to Japan.

Two years later, in 1920, Japan became a founding member of the League of Nations. The League's primary goals included peace among nations, settling disputes through discussion instead of war, and total disarmament. A council of four nations—Japan, Great Britain, France, and Italy—led the League. Japan was pleased to hold a leadership position.

The Regent Takes Over

By 1921, it had become obvious that the Taisho emperor was mentally unfit to lead the country. Young Prince Hirohito became regent. A regent is a person appointed to rule when the current ruler is too young, too sick, or otherwise unable to govern. Japan's political leaders wanted Japan's citizens to see Hirohito as a dynamic, vigorous young man. Thus, his advisers expected Hirohito to participate in army maneuvers, listen to lectures, exercise, and study French.

During the first years of Prince Hirohito's regency, Japan struggled through a period of economic uncertainty. Businesses closed and employees found themselves out of work. In rural districts of Japan, tenant farmers united against what they considered their oppressive landlords. The tenants began a series of rotating strikes during which a certain landlord's crops were left rotting in the fields, thus causing the landlord to lose money. By choosing to target only one landlord in a region at a time, tenant farmers were still able to earn money, and only the selected landlord would lose income.

The economy of Japan had seemed to recover. Then, in 1923, a devastating earthquake struck the cities of Tokyo and Yokohama, as well as their surrounding districts. The earthquake, called the Great Kanto Earthquake, destroyed more than half of Tokyo and left more than two and a half million people without homes.

Reactions in the Military

Throughout the Taisho era, the Japanese military continued to develop its plans for expansion. The successful expulsion of Germany from China had proven Japan's military strength. Military leaders intended to make China the next Japanese colony. Japan had plans to add the Asian nation of Indonesia to its holdings too. Japanese diplomats indicated Japan's desires to annex land and made it clear that Japan's army and navy would back up Japan's threats.

Treaties signed in 1921 and 1922 had limited the size of Japan's military. As part of the Five-Power Naval Arms Limitation Treaty, France, Great Britain, the United States, Italy, and Japan promised to reduce the number of warships in their navies. Japan was required to limit its ships to 60 percent of the U.S. total. This limited navy was unacceptable to Japan's military leaders.

The Japanese military continued to intrude in government policies. According to the military, Russia was Japan's biggest threat. Concerns over China continued, and China held a place on Japan's list of major enemies. Expectations of trouble on the Asian continent led the Japanese army to expand its military presence in Manchuria and Korea and to continue to train its increasingly larger army.

Contrary to the wishes of military officials, Japanese leaders adopted a new national defense plan in 1923. The Cabinet decided to reduce the troop presence in China as well as cut Japan's military budget. The size of Japan's army

The Modern Japanese Woman

Up until the Meiji era, Japanese women worked only at home. Hiring a woman to work as a secretary or a salesperson was simply not done. In 1894, a Japanese businessman visited a department store in Pennsylvania and saw women working there. He took this idea back to Japan with him and hired several young women to work for him.

This idea of hiring women eventually spread throughout Japan. Women began working in city stores and offices and as teachers and nurses. Some went to work in factories. These women worked the same hours and performed the same jobs as Japanese men, but they earned less than half the wages men earned. Further, most women who worked in Japan's textile factories were forced to live in near prisonlike conditions.

To put a stop to practices such as these, and to achieve equal rights and pay, some Japanese women joined trade unions. These women wanted better conditions, better pay, and greater freedom. According to historian Andrew Gordon, "This was part of a struggle among some women … to live what they called 'human' lives. … They sought minimal freedom and respect for themselves and their contributions to their families or to their nation."[1]

[1]Andrew Gordon, *A Modern History of Japan: From Tokugawa Times to the Present* (New York: Oxford University Press, 2003), 151.

Some women worked as weavers in the early 1900s. The working conditions in such jobs were very poor.

The Great Kanto Earthquake, and the fires that spread in its aftermath, destroyed Tokyo's Kanda District in 1923.

The Great Kanto Earthquake

Just before noon on September 1, 1923, a massive earthquake shook the cities of Tokyo and Yokohama. Centered southwest of Tokyo, the quake measured 8.3 on the Richter scale. As a result of the quake, a tidal wave swept over the coastline. In the aftermath of the quake, kitchen fires caused by the disaster spread, ultimately burning down more than half of Tokyo.

The damage and property loss added up to nearly the equivalent of $1 billion. In addition to the quake, Yokohama experienced a tidal wave and a flood of burning oil that poured through its city streets. Fourteen major Japanese towns showed serious damage from the quake, along with 600 miles (960 km) of railroad tracks.

Because of the earthquake, Prince Hirohito delayed his marriage to Princess Nagako. Eventually, in 1924, they did wed. The couple traveled through the once earthquake-ravaged streets of Tokyo, cheered by crowds lining their route.

The greatest cost from the earthquake was the loss of human lives. Nearly two hundred thousand people died from the quake. Another three hundred thousand to five hundred thousand people suffered injuries.

was dramatically reduced to make way for modernized weapons and a sweeping reorganization of Japan's military. The navy scrapped old warships and replaced them with more modern planes and submarines.

Young Japanese military officers despised the cuts to personnel and to the budget. They believed that these actions weakened Japan's image. Military discipline became lax, and both soldiers and lower-ranking officers became openly rebellious. Army minister Tanaka Giichi said that soldiers had "become bold and rebellious in their attitudes, and criminal acts have increased, especially cases where men form small groups and act violently."[17]

Efforts were made to instill a greater sense of nationalism among Japan's soldiers by training the men to follow rules and regulations and to obey, without question, the orders of their superior officers. Unfortunately, the Japanese people voiced their opinions once again through protests and riots. The critical attitudes expressed in the streets of Japan found their way into the military's barracks. Common soldiers openly questioned the politics and policies of Japan's government leaders—and even its emperor.

Many officers began to follow the teachings of Tanaka Chigaku, who en-

Japanese nationalism was strong in the early 1920s. Children carried Japanese flags to show their pride, even in the countryside.

couraged Japanese citizens to embrace *kokuchukai*—nationalism at its most pure. Tanaka believed in nationalism and anticipated global peace only when Japan dominated all of Asia and much of the rest of the world.

Some of Tanaka's followers joined the Japanese military. They attended military schools and became officers in the Japan-ese army and navy. Slowly, members of the kokuchukai movement rose through the military ranks, attaining positions of importance in the military's hierarchy. It might seem that having patriotic, nation-alistic officers would be a good thing, but Japan needed nationalism tempered with good judgment. Instead, kokuchukai fol-lowers tended more toward extremism.

Chapter Four

Upheaval at Home and Abroad

After serving five years as regent, Hirohito became emperor on December 25, 1926, when his father died. It took two years before Hirohito's official enthronement ceremony took place. Part of the delay was due to the long period of national mourning for his father, the Taisho Emperor. The rest of the delay was because the Japanese people had doubts about their new monarch. A two-year campaign of events, ceremonies, newspaper articles, and photo opportunities remade the quiet, reserved Hirohito into a noble emperor—the type of emperor the Japanese people wanted.

Hirohito's enthronement events required great preparation, and the equivalent of $7,360,000 was spent on them. Hirohito chose the name *Showa*, which means "bright peace," for his reign. Ironically, the early years of Hirohito's reign were troubled with one crisis after another, both at home and abroad.

The ritual and ceremonies that took place during Hirohito's enthronement were public displays of the emperor's newfound popularity. Hundreds of thousands of Japanese citizens dined at banquets in honor of the new emperor, attended parades, and received awards. Thousands of criminals received government pardons and were released from prison. Even children took part in the events, marching through the cities of Japan and waving Japanese flags.

The formal enthronement ceremonies began on November 6, 1928, with a royal procession from Tokyo to Kyoto. Hirohito addressed the people:

I sincerely wish to bring harmony to the people by kindheartedly guiding them to the good, thus promoting the further prosperity of the country. Externally I sincerely wish to maintain eternal world peace and advance goodwill among nations through diplomacy, thus contributing to the welfare of humanity. You, our subjects, join cooperatively with one another, put aside self-interest, and take on service to the public, thereby allowing me to nurture the great legacy of my divine ancestors and respond to the spirit of their benevolence.[18]

The most significant events connected to Hirohito's ascension to the throne involved Japan's military. In Tokyo, Hirohito watched hour after hour as thousands of troops paraded before their new ruler. In Yokohama, the Japanese navy brought out their fleet, putting submarines, war planes, and aircraft carriers on display. This was the real measure of Hirohito's importance to the nation. He was now the ultimate commander of the Imperial Japanese Army and navy.

Problems at Home

The more than seven million dollars spent on Hirohito's enthronement added to the burdens Japanese citizens faced. During the previous year, the economy had struggled. Many Japanese lost money when banks failed in 1927. Businesses struggled to make ends meet. Many were forced to close their doors, putting thousands of Japanese citizens out of work. In Japan's rural districts, too, tenant farmers and landlords battled over rents, prices, and financial losses.

As Japan's economy suffered, world events brought even more trouble to the nation. In 1929, the New York Stock Market suffered its worst crash of stock prices in history. This led to the Great Depression, a period of several years during which banks closed, individuals lost their savings, and working-class people lost their jobs. The Great Depression affected nations throughout the world. In Japan, the economy relied heavily on exports to Western nations. During the Great Depression, purchases of high-priced goods stopped. Japan's foreign market disappeared. This affected all aspects of Japan's economy, from the powerful industrial families to the peasants working in the rice and barley fields.

Although Japan's *zaibatsu* (large, family-owned businesses) appeared to dominate Japan's economy, the true foundation was the small businesses. Tokyo, Yokohama, Kyoto, and other Japanese cities depended on small, privately owned retail shops to supply Japanese citizens with goods. Restaurants, teashops, butchers, sandal makers, laundries, and hundreds of other small businesses kept Japan's cities alive. These businesses depended on small profits to stay afloat. When those profits disappeared, the owners faced bankruptcy or complete financial ruin. In Tokyo during the Great Depression,

Emperor Hirohito's 1928 enthronement cost more than $7,000,000.

retail failures doubled in just four years.

Small business owners formed associations in an effort to slow the effects of the economic depression. These associations called on the Japanese government for action. Other than loans that the businesses would never be able to repay, the business owners got absolutely no help from the government. According to the Imperial Middle Class Federated Alliance, small business owners felt that politicians and big business owners had betrayed them by "trampling the middle class of commercial, industrial, and agricultural producers."[19]

Radicals took a socialistic view of the economy. They believed that the government should bail out all failing businesses and distribute wealth and opportunity equally among the Japanese people. Conservatives in Japan wanted reform, but only if it did not reduce their wealth and power. Government officials summarized the conservative view in this way:

> The political parties, the zaibatsu, and a small privileged group attached to the ruling classes … pursue their own egotistic interests and desires, to the neglect of national defence and to the confusion of government. As a result,

In 1934, Japanese schoolgirls pounded rice to help make the rice cakes that were used to feed the poor in Tokyo.

national dignity is lost abroad, while at home the morale of the people collapses; the villages are exhausted, and medium and small industry and commerce have been driven to the wall.[20]

When Japanese employers laid off workers, the unemployed headed back to their former villages. The farms they returned to could not provide work for so many workers. Many of the jobless found themselves living off their relatives. Prices for rice, barley, and other produce dropped. A crop failure in northern Japan added to the serious financial problems for tenant farmers and landlords alike.

The landlords in Japan thought that they could make more money by doing their own labor. Family members who had once left for city jobs would now return and begin to work in the landlords' fields. The landlords would then reap the profits. Tenant farmers already working these landlords' fields, however, disagreed. They had contracts giving them the right to farm specific tracts of land. To protect their interests, many tenant farmers raised fences around their land and posted guards to prevent landlords from taking back the land. Some tenant farmers protested their treatment by the landlords in rallies, while others took part, once again, in riots.

Patriotic Societies

The financial woes of the Great Depression did have one positive effect on Japan's nationalism: the Japanese people banded together to overcome their problems. Japanese citizens looked to the past, to traditional days when *kokutai* (national pride) brought peace and prosperity to Japan. Those Japanese citizens who believed in tradition remained loyal to the emperor and resented Hirohito's critics. This intense nationalism drew people together. They began to form patriotic societies. In these societies, conservative thinkers joined with military leaders in groups that pledged to restore Japan to greatness. Membership in these societies more than doubled from 1932 to 1936. These groups took on symbolic titles, such as the Cherry Blossom Society (Sakura Kai) or the Imperial Way. Sakura Kai referred to the cherry blossom, a symbol of a bright future, while the Imperial Way represented loyalty to the emperor.

These societies called for rebuilding the government and, therefore, the economy. They hoped to restore the concept of a rich and powerful Japan, built on military strength and respect for authority, namely to the emperor. Nationalistic groups despised big business and wealthy executives, and they hoped to rid Japan of foreigners, who had modern views and corrupt thinking. Patriotic societies believed in

Many Japanese who could not find jobs in the city went back to their family farms.

Japan's destiny as the supreme leader of Asia. They believed that the road to this destiny was a strong military. Not surprisingly, many young, impressionable Japanese army officers joined these societies. The members of the Sakura Kai and the Imperial Way would achieve the dreams of their nation.

While the patriotic societies may have viewed Hirohito as godlike, government officials certainly did not. In 1930, the Minseito, or Democratic Party, held the most power. Prime Minister Hamaguchi Osachi wanted to cut military spending, which would be in keeping with agreements made between Japan and other world powers. A member of a patriotic society put an end to Hamaguchi's plan by attacking him. Hamaguchi's wounds did not kill him immediately, but he died by the end of the year. The next prime minister did not make the same mistake as Hamaguchi. He gave way to right-wing demands.

Military Actions

While tensions grew at home, a group of young officers in Manchuria decided to take action. Manchuria's value to Japan was significant. Japan needed the region for its natural resources and produce. Manchuria provided Japan with oil, coal, iron, soybeans, and tobacco. Japanese factories in the region spun silk and cotton. In total, there were nearly eight hundred Japanese-owned factories in Manchuria that Japan had to keep secure.

Sakura Kai

Sakura Kai, or the Cherry Blossom Society, was a secret organization founded by officers of the Imperial Japanese Army. The group opposed the current government structure and wanted to replace democracy in Japan with a one-party system run by the military. If necessary, they were willing to use a military coup d'etat to oust Japan's government officials.

The two leaders of Sakura Kai were Lieutenant Colonel Hashimoto Kingoro and Captain Cho Isamu. Sakura Kai began with only ten members, all Japanese military officers. By 1931, the society had fifty members.

Sakura Kai members made two attempts to overthrow the Japanese government. The March Incident of 1931 was the first. It began with a plan that called for massive riots in Tokyo, so that all Japanese troops would be called into the city. Once the army arrived, Sakura Kai would take over government offices. A new cabinet would be formed under the leadership of General Ugaki, Japan's war minister. The plot failed. Six months later, Sakura Kai attempted another military coup with the Imperial Colors Incident. Sakura Kai's leaders were arrested before they could put this plan into effect, and the society was forced to break up.

The Kwantung Army, Japan's army in Manchuria, began an aggressive plan to expand Japan's hold over the region. On September 18, 1931, Kwantung Army troops blew up a stretch of railroad tracks outside the Manchurian city of Mukden. The army quickly blamed the Chinese for the explosion and swooped into Mukden to protect Japan's interests. The Kwantung Army then attacked Chinese troops in the region, forcing the Chinese to retreat until Japan controlled most of southern Manchuria.

The leaders of the Kwantung Army had acted without orders. Japanese government officials were outraged by this obvious act of aggression. These government officials hid their anger well, however. It was hard to punish the Kwantung Army troops for an incident that brought such joy to the Japanese people. Newspapers and radio broadcasts applauded the action as a means of relieving Japan's unemployment problem and securing Japan's access to Manchuria's natural resources. The Justice Ministry called the Manchurian Incident, as it came to be known, a "divine wind."[21]

Emperor Hirohito disagreed with the actions of the Kwantung Army. He ordered the army to stop its aggression and not to move deeper into Manchuria. Japan's prime minister claimed that the

Manchuria and Surrounding Areas

In 1932, Japan turned the territory of Manchuria into the country of Manchukuo.

order had come too late—Japanese troops were already flooding from Korea into Manchuria to support the Kwantung Army. The Kwantung Army continued its advance, taking over much of northern Manchuria and all land up to the Great Wall of China.

China made a formal complaint about Japan's aggression to the League of Nations in October 1931. The League examined Japan's actions in China and drafted a resolution demanding that Japan return the areas of Manchuria it had taken during the Manchurian Incident. Such a resolution required a unanimous vote by the League's members. Japan vetoed the proposed resolution, so the matter of Japan returning the lands to China ended with no action taken against Japan.

Manchukuo

In February 1932, Japan announced its intentions to form an independent nation in Manchuria, called Manchukuo. The new country included all the land the Kwantung Army had annexed and some land they had yet to conquer. According to Japan, this new nation was being formed at the request of Manchuria's citizens.

Japan chose a puppet leader, or a ruler controlled by others, to rule Manchukuo. P'u Yi (1906–1967) was selected by Japan as Manchukuo's new leader. P'u Yi had

The Kwantung Army

The Kwantung Army was a military unit in the Imperial Japanese Army from 1906 to 1945. On the surface, the Kwantung Army reported directly to the Japanese high command in Tokyo. In reality, the unit's officers were rebellious and took actions without regard to Japanese foreign policy or military orders. The Kwantung Army was responsible for the Manchurian Incident and the takeover of Manchuria.

During World War II, large parts of the unit were transferred from Manchuria to islands in the Pacific. In 1945, when Soviet forces invaded Manchuria, the Kwantung Army's troops numbered six hundred thousand. The Kwantung Army's orders were to form a line of resistance between the invading Soviet forces and the city of Hsinking. Weeks later, the Kwantung Army was forced to surrender on orders from the Japanese emperor, but there was little remaining of the original Kwantung Army. Many Kwantung troops had been killed in skirmishes with the Soviets. Others were sent to work in prisoner-of-war camps. At the end of World War II, the once-powerful Kwantung Army was no more.

once been emperor of China but had been living in exile for a number of years. On the surface, Manchukuo appeared to have a full range of Chinese and Manchurian leaders, but each leader had a Japanese adviser guiding his actions. The Japanese advisers pulled the puppet strings, and Manchukuo's officials followed along. There was nothing independent about the supposedly independent nation of Manchukuo.

Again, China complained to the League of Nations about Japan's actions. The League planned to openly criticize Japan, but Japan, having no intention of giving up its hard-won land in Manchuria, immediately resigned from the League. The Japanese people applauded Japan's resignation, but several Japanese officials realized that problems might follow from such an action. Said Makino Nobuaki, the Japanese Keeper of the Privy Seal,

> The people act as if by withdrawing [from the League of Nations] we have achieved something great, or they believe our achievement is withdrawal itself. And the media rush about ... [trying to realize] that goal. All of this shows the shallowness of thought in the Japanese public.[22]

Assassinations

Throughout the 1930s, Japan's military continued to advance its influence on Japan and Japanese politics. The people did not complain because they saw the military as a symbol of Japan's international status. Through the military, Japan would become and would remain a great power.

The Japanese military then broke into several distinct factions, or groups, each with its own plan to achieve this greatness. The older, more senior officers held rank in the War Ministry, the navy, and the general staff. Senior officers wanted to advance Japan's military through improved, modern equipment. The Tosei-ha, or Control Faction, led these senior officers. The Tosei-ha included the chief of the general staff, the war minister, and the inspector general of military education. The Control Faction believed that tanks, submarines, and warplanes could win battles more easily than ground troops alone. With this modern equipment, the Control Faction felt it could reduce the number of troops the Japanese military needed.

Young officers who worked on the front lines made up another faction. These men believed that defending Japan and its policies was their duty. They preferred nationalism to politics and were not opposed to using violence to achieve their goals. This faction was called the Kodo-ha, or Imperial Way. Traditional values of training, loyalty, and military power were key principles of the Imperial Way.

While all the military factions believed in creating a stronger Japan, the means by which they wanted to achieve this goal differed. In 1931, members of Sakura Kai planned a string of assassinations

The Last Chinese Emperor

The last emperor of China, P'u Yi, belonged to the Qing dynasty. He was a direct descendant of the Manchu, a family of nomads from Manchuria. Born in 1906, P'u Yi was named to the throne by his grandmother. At the time, P'u Yi was not quite three years old, so his father served as his regent.

During P'u Yi's reign, China experienced great upheaval. In 1912, the five-year-old emperor was forced to give up his throne. He remained in seclusion in the Forbidden City in Beijing. P'u Yi was raised by government officials and court ladies. In 1917, he became emperor again due to the efforts of a Chinese warlord. The warlord restored the Chinese empire, but this restoration was short lived. In 1924, P'u Yi was again removed from the throne and this time exiled from the Forbidden City.

In 1932, the Japanese chose P'u Yi as their puppet leader in Manchukuo. He held this position until the Japanese surrendered at the end of World War II. P'u Yi spent four years under house arrest in the Soviet Union, then nine years in a Chinese labor camp. He died as a commoner at the age of sixty-one.

designed to put their favorite leaders into office. Their attempt in March of that year failed when several officers decided to back out of their agreement. Then in October 1931, authorities stopped a second attempt. Leaders of Sakura Kai were arrested, but they received minimal punishments. Many Japanese people believed that these men had acted out of patriotism. In Japan, assassination in the name of patriotism was acceptable.

Japanese troops enter Manchuria following the 1931 bombing of the railway near Shenyang, beginning 14 years of conflict between China and Japan.

In 1932, more radical groups embarked on a series of assassinations that proved more successful than Sakura Kai's attempts had been. Japan's former minister of finance and a zaibatsu executive were both assassinated. In May, a group of naval officers led a rampage against government officials, killing Prime Minister Inukai Tsuyoshi, among others. Politics in Japan had become deadly business.

Attacks continued, pitting political groups against self-proclaimed patriots and one military faction against another. In 1935, Aizawa Suburo, a lieutenant colonel in the Imperial Way faction, assassinated Japan's new inspector general of military education. The new inspector had replaced a man that Aizawa had supported. Aizawa assassinated the inspector general with a sword, stabbing him through the back. Members of the Control Faction demanded that Aizawa be arrested and tried for this murder.

At the trial, the justices allowed Aizawa to use the witness stand as a pulpit for spouting off against government corruption and greedy business leaders. Although he pleaded guilty to murder, he gave the excuse that he had been performing his duty to his emperor. Aizawa ranted on about how those close to the emperor filled the emperor's mind with lies based on their own interests. The defense lawyer warned the court, "If the court fails to understand the spirit which guided Colonel Aizawa, a second Aizawa, and even a third, will appear."[23] This prophecy came true in 1936.

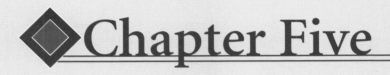

Chapter Five

1936—A Pivotal Year

Japan was a nation torn in half. Parts of Japan had modernized and westernized. Other parts remained feudal and traditional. In Tokyo, the Ginza—the shopping and entertainment district—glowed red and gold and green from the lights of cafés, movie theaters, and stylish fashion shops. Men wore suits, ties, and slouch hats, while the women dressed in the latest dresses and fur coats from Paris and London. A few blocks away, men and women moved through narrow alleys dressed in the traditional Japanese dress of kimonos and sandals. Teashops and geisha (hostess) houses retained Japan's ancient heritage. People traveled on foot or in rickshaws (bicycle-pulled carts).

Farther still from Tokyo's center, farmers lived in poverty. Their crops did not sell. Their families starved. Fathers wrote to their sons, telling them of hard times. Those sons had left their farms to join Japan's army. Frustration grew among young officers in the military as they observed the greed and power of Japan's wealthy businessmen and the corruption of its politicians. Thoughts of relatives starving fed these soldiers' anger. As the population in Japan grew, the gap between poverty and wealth increased.

The State of Japan

One of Japan's greatest problems in the 1930s was its population. Japan's four main islands had a combined population of more than eighty million people. The population grew steadily at a rate of one million new Japanese citizens per year. Such a large population strained the nation's natural resources, agriculture, and economy.

The Great Depression increased the stress on Japan's economy. Banks did not have enough cash to cover the money people had deposited. Businesses closed

their factories, putting people out of work. Jobless people could not buy new goods or pay their bank loans. More businesses closed, and more banks failed.

The zaibatsu, Japan's major employers, could not sell their exports and closed mines and factories. Japanese workers lost their jobs and had no money to spend on products. Prices on farm goods dropped, and farmers could barely afford to sell their produce.

The downward cycle of the Japanese economy led to a rise in left-wing political parties and trade unions. Nationalist leaders tried to silence the rumblings of discontent coming from radical activists. Kita Ikki, a popular nationalist author and politician, called for reform measures that would return Japan to its traditional values. Kita claimed, "the Japanese are following the destructive examples of the Western nations."[24]

Changing the Government

Kita's ideas became exceedingly popular among radicals and imperialists alike. Both sides wanted change, and Kita made recommendations to strengthen Japan and its position in Asia. Kita suggested that voting be restricted to male heads of households. He believed the emperor

In the 1930s, the Ginza district of Tokyo was the retail center of the city, featuring numerous boutiques, shops, and restaurants.

should rid himself of corrupt businessmen and politicians. He called for the reduction or elimination of the powers of the Diet and the Cabinet. Kita took a vaguely socialist approach to industry, recommending that key industries be owned and operated by the government and personal wealth be limited to only one million yen. Women, claimed Kita, should return to the business of running the home, arranging flowers, and being submissive to their husbands' rule.

Japan had a history of changing its leadership through assassination. Early in the seventeenth century, *gekokujo*— "the lower commanding the upper"— became an acceptable means of ridding the people of corrupt or inept rulers. The Japanese understood the motivation of people who tried to help the nation in this way. The Aizawa Incident of August 12, 1935, had been an excellent example of gekokujo. Lieutenant Aizawa Saburo assassinated Major General Nagata Tetsuzan because Nagata had replaced a leader Aizawa had supported.

Poverty, starvation, corrupt politicians, wealth in the hands of a few, and unwanted Western influences united young Japanese army officers against the government. Secret societies arose among these disgruntled officers. Previous attempts to overthrow the government and place Japan under a military dictatorship had failed, but the Japanese people felt that such attempts were honorable, and they expected them. Usually, successful political assassins became heroes in Japan.

Zaibatsu

Zaibatsu were family businesses that rose to national prominence during the Meiji era. Most began as small enterprises founded by wealthy families, although that was not true of the Okura zaibatsu. That family began as peasants selling groceries and moved beyond foodstuffs to weapons just before the start of the Meiji Restoration.

The three zaibatsu that dominated the Japanese market were Mitsubishi, Mitsui, and Sumitomo. During the Showa era, the Mitsui Bank served as Japan's major bank. The Yasuda family founded another bank, the Third National Bank of Japan. Mitsubishi became a power in the shipping industry with the help of loans secured from the government. Sumitomo began as an iron smelting operation and moved into buying and selling copper. The Furukawa and Kuhara zaibatsu made their money in mining.

Gekokujo

Snow blanketed Tokyo on the morning of February 26, 1936. Before dawn, the leaders of what had to be one of the boldest coups d'état of the government in Japanese history gathered their troops. In all, fifteen hundred officers and infantrymen took part in the event that came to be known as the February 26 Incident.

On the surface, the plan was simple: assassinate current and former government leaders and advisers and replace them with military officers. The prime target was Japan's prime minister, Okada Keisuke. Others on the hit list included the finance minister, the Keeper of the Privy Seal, the inspector general of military education, and Prince Saionji Kinmochi, one of Hirohito's closest advisers and the last of the *genro* (elder statesmen).

At five o'clock in the morning, troops burst into the home of Prime Minister Okada. At the time, Okada and his brother-in-law, Matsuo Denzo, were both sleeping in the home. Hearing the commotion, the men rose and slipped into a side room. As the rebels moved through the house, Matsuo confronted them. The troops mistook Matsuo for the prime minister and killed Matsuo in the hallway. An officer mistakenly identified Matsuo's body as the prime minister's, and the troops headed on to their next victim. Okada fled into a servant's room and hid in a cabinet under a pile of dirty laundry.

The first motorized vehicles began rolling off the production line at Japan's Mazda factory in 1937.

70 Samurai, Shoguns, and Soldiers: The Rise of the Japanese Military

One of the prime minister's secretaries called the local police, only to find that the police station in Tokyo's Imperial Zone had been taken over by the rebels. Bursts of machine gun fire sounded throughout the area that contained the Imperial Palace, the Diet, and other major government officials' homes.

At the home of Japan's finance minister, a lieutenant and his men broke down the door. The finance minister lay sleeping. The lieutenant found the finance minister and shot him repeatedly. Officers then slashed the finance minister with their swords, leaving his bloody corpse on the floor. Rumors claim that the officers then apologized to the finance minister's wife for causing such an annoyance in her home.

The attempt on Prince Saionji's life failed. The officer in charge hesitated to commit a violent act against the last of the genro. Prince Saionji, upon hearing of the mass assassinations taking place, decided not to wait to see if he was on the hit list. He left his home and fled to a hiding place where one hundred police guarded him.

These assassin troops, called mustards because of their uniforms' yellowish color, spared no one. The Keeper of the Privy Seal, one of Hirohito's advisers, died from machine gun fire. Mustards killed

A former admiral in the Japanese Imperial Navy, Prime Minister Okada Keisuke survived the assassination attempt of February 26, 1936, but resigned from office two days later.

the inspector general of military education, and the emperor's grand chamberlain suffered severe wounds as well.

The assassinations were over before most Japanese had risen to go to work. The government center of Tokyo lay under control of the rebel officers. Tokyo was paralyzed. Phones did not work, streetcars did not pick up passengers, and businesses in the government zone did not open. The outside world knew nothing about the attempted coup, since the rebels stopped telegrams, overseas cables, and radio broadcasts from spreading the news.

The rebels distributed their manifesto, a public statement of a political group's reasons and principles, to the news media. Although the police tried to stop its publication, several members of the press got hold of copies. The following is an excerpt from the rebels' manifesto:

The national essence (*kokutai*) of Japan, as a land of the gods, exists in the fact that the Emperor reigns with undiminished power from time immemorial into the farthest future in order that the natural beauty of the country may be propagated through the universe, so that all men under the sun may be able to enjoy their lives to the fullest extent…

In recent years, however, there have appeared many persons whose chief aim and purpose have been to

Reporters and journalists continued to produce daily newspaper reports despite the chaos occurring outside their office following the events of February 26, 1936.

amass personal material wealth, disregarding the general welfare and prosperity of the Japanese people, with the result that the sovereignty of the Emperor has been greatly impaired. The people of Japan have suffered deeply as a result of this tendency and many vexing issues now confronting Japan are attributable to this fact.

The *genro*, the senior statesmen, military cliques, plutocrats, bureaucrats, and political parties are all traitors who are destroying the national essence.[25]

Prime Minister Okada, having been found safe in the cabinet under the laundry by loyal guards, arrived at the Imperial Palace looking worn out from his experience. Hirohito was relieved that the prime minister had escaped assassination.

Meanwhile, in the Japanese War Office, generals debated what to do about the uprising. They did not want to openly oppose the rebels, nor did they want to allow the rebels to get away with murder. They did, however, understand the thought behind the coup. For the most part, the generals chose to do nothing in response. Hirohito, on the other hand, was not so reluctant to become involved.

The rebels claimed to be fulfilling their duty to the emperor by assassinating government leaders. Hirohito decided to end the rebellion quickly. Acting at Hirohito's request, General Kashii issued the following statement: "Orders to establish an emergency guard over conditions in Tokyo have been issued to the First Division. By command of the emperor, I have ordered mobilization of a portion of my troops at important points, the purpose of which is to maintain order in the capital and to protect important objects. ... I hope both officials and the people will avoid spreading wild rumors and will cooperate in the maintenance of peace."[26]

A second, somewhat bizarre order placed Tokyo's government district under the control of the First Division. The rebel troops belonged to this division. This order was designed to make the rebel troops feel as though they were actually following the emperor's orders.

Negotiators arrived to discuss conditions under which the rebels would give up and to remind the troops that the emperor had ordered their surrender. A radio announcer went on the air, telling the rebel troops to follow Hirohito's orders: "If you continue to resist, you will be traitors for disobeying the Emperor's order. ... Your past crimes will be forgiven. Your fathers and brothers, as well as the entire nation, sincerely pray that you do this. Immediately leave your present positions and come back."[27]

Then, slowly, a few rebels deserted their posts, followed by others, until the rebellion had come to an end. One officer,

Captain Nonaka Shiro, chose to do what samurai did when they lost face—he committed seppuku. He left behind a note:

In recent years, the sins of the traitors at home have been redeemed by the blood of our comrades in Manchuria and Shanghai. What answer can I give to the souls of these men if I spend the rest of my days in vain here in the capital? Am I insane or am I a fool? There is but one road for me to take."[28]

Three days after the assassinations began, the rebellion came to an end. The majority of the rebel troops returned to their posts and suffered no serious punishment. The officers who had led the coup did not fare as well. They were arrested and tried for acts of murder and treason.

Martial Law

After the February 26 Incident ended, the Japanese government declared martial law. As head of the military, Emperor Hirohito began wearing military uniforms daily. At the emperor's request, a court-martial convened to hear the trials of the rebellious officers.

These trials were held under strict secrecy. The defendants did not have lawyers representing them. All power lay in the hands of the justice of the court. The court found all seventeen defendants guilty and sentenced them to death by firing squad. The court findings and

Emperor Hirohito

Hirohito (1901–1989) was the son of the Taisho emperor and the grandson of Emperor Meiji. At the age of eleven, Hirohito was formally named heir to the throne.

In 1926, Hirohito became the 124th emperor of Japan. He named his reign *Showa* (bright peace). Ironically, Japan enjoyed little peace during Hirohito's reign. Japan went to war against China and, later, allied itself with Germany and Italy in World War II.

Hirohito was not a typical emperor. He would have preferred being a marine biologist to being the ruler of Japan. He broke with tradition by walking around the palace in torn trousers and ragged jackets. He represented in some ways the ideal monarch: humble, frugal, compassionate, and generous. Science and the Western world sparked his interest. It is said that when he died in 1989, Hirohito was buried with two of his favorite possessions: his microscope and a Mickey Mouse watch.

death sentences were given in the middle of the night to keep the fate of the rebel officers secret.

Carrying out the execution by firing squad of people considered heroes by the Japanese populace made government officials nervous. They decided to test the waters by executing political assassin Aizawa Saburo two weeks before the scheduled execution of the February 26 Incident's rebels. Aizawa's last words were, "It is proper that a soldier should die to the sound of rifles. Flesh disintegrates but the soul lives on. Seven, even eight lives more will I devote to this imperial land."[29] Aizawa's execution passed without incident.

According to the sentences handed down, fifteen army officers who took part in the February 26 Incident faced the firing squad. Two other men who had been sentenced to death for their part in the rebellion were spared, though the reasons for this were never explained.

Repercussions

All aspects of the trial and executions of the participants in the February 26 Incident had been kept secret, but the War Office felt the need to explain the actions of the rebels. It released the contents of their manifesto to be published in national and local newspapers.

In the manifesto, the officers stated that they despised the corruption dominating Japanese society at the time and the weaknesses shown by the Japanese people for all things Western and, there-

German-Japanese Anti-Comintern Pact

The Comintern, or Communist International, was founded in 1919. It was an international organization dedicated to promoting communism, a system of government in which all factories, farms, and natural resources are owned by the community as a whole, throughout the world. The Comintern held seven world conferences to discuss worker states that followed Communist principles. It was a primary goal of the Comintern to convert capitalist societies, such as Japan, into Communist societies.

On November 25, 1936, Japan formed the Anti-Comintern Pact with Germany. An imperial Japanese ambassador and a German ambassador signed the document in Berlin, Germany. The two governments agreed to share information about Communist Party activities in their own countries with one another. Both felt that the Comintern's goal endangered peace and social welfare in their own countries and throughout the world and could bring economic ruin. This agreement was the first sign to the rest of the world that Japan and Germany had become allies.

fore, corrupt. They opposed the rise of Japanese millionaires while other citizens lived in poverty. They stated that earlier Japanese cabinets gave in too easily to Western demands regarding Japan's buildup of its navy and army, and this was an act of cowardice. They believed such acts caused Japan to lose face among other nations.

The officers suggested that advisers close to the emperor had done the nation a disservice by interfering with the emperor's rights as a national and military leader. Finally, the rebels had hoped to restore Japan on the road to military power and expansion. They felt this would make Japan the dominant power throughout East Asia, which the officers thought was appropriate and justified.

The Japanese people did not see the actions of the February 26 Incident as evil. Other army officers agreed that the army and navy should grow and dominate the region. Many civilians shared the officers' resentment over the rise of millionaires. The entire population of Japan, not only the February 26 rebels, had condemned Japanese leaders who agreed to Western demands that weakened Japan's standing as a world power. Few Japanese disagreed with Japan's destiny and right as the ruler of East Asia.

The government's reactions to the February 26 Incident were not surprising. Japan embarked on an expansion plan that would lead the nation even farther

FIFTEEN CENTS

February 24, 1936

TIME

The Weekly Newsmagazine

International, Sovfoto, Wide World

Volume XXVII

**JAPANESE EMPEROR
MOSCOW SECRETARY**

**MANCHU EMPEROR
NANKING PREMIER**

Number 8

*The Spokesman: "One false step—one mistake—will go bang like a
firecracker."* (See FOREIGN NEWS)

Circulation Office, 330 East 22nd Street, Chicago.   (Reg. U. S. Pat. Off.)   Editorial and Advertising Offices, 135 East 42nd Street, New York.

Circulation this issue more than 600,000

76   Samurai, Shoguns, and Soldiers: The Rise of the Japanese Military

into China. The government tried to curb the growth of communism by entering into an alliance with Germany—the Japanese-German Anti-Comintern Pact of 1936. The February 26 Incident did not completely eliminate the corruption surrounding the throne, but the goals of that event encouraged the rise of fascism, a political movement that favors a government run by a dictator who eliminates all opposition. Japan turned its attention to mobilizing its army and navy and preparing for war on a global scale.

The February 24, 1936, cover of Time Magazine featured portraits of four influential Asian leaders—(clockwise from top left) Emperor Hirohito of Japan, Manchukuo Emperor P'u Yi, Chinese general Chiang Kai-shek, and Soviet leader Joseph Stalin.

Chapter Six

The Storm Breaks

After the February 26 Incident, politicians became extremely reluctant to offend Japan's military. As 1937 began, Prime Minister Hirota Koki favored the military to such an extent that the Diet became disillusioned with his leadership. Members of opposing parties accused the Cabinet of being slaves to the wishes of military officials. Already, the military's budget seemed large. It would only increase if Hirota did not curb military spending.

Insults flew across the aisles of the Diet and tempers flared. Representative Hamada Kunimatsu, angered by insults from a war minister, said, "I will kill myself by hara-kiri if it can be proved that the Army and the Cabinet are not hand in glove."[30] With the Diet against him, Hirota resigned as Japan's prime minister.

Emperor Hirohito's adviser, Prince Saionji, wanted another military officer, General Ugaki Kazushige, to succeed Hirota as prime minister. The military's Control Faction rejected Ugaki because in years past he had reduced the size of the army. The Control Faction wanted a hawk—a prowar, promilitary prime minister—and claimed they could not find anyone willing to work with Ugaki. A somewhat embarrassed Ugaki returned to the emperor and admitted he could not form a government. He said, "I am partly responsible for the present condition in the Army, which has become a political organization. I feel sorry for the Emperor because of this state of affairs. Moreover, I greatly regret that the Army, which I have loved so long, has been brought to such a pass."[31]

A different general then became prime minister, mostly because he was not opposed to the army's Control Faction. Japanese politics had turned into a war zone, with the Diet on one side and the army on the other. The army approved of the new prime minister, but the Diet did not. The new prime minister resigned after only four months in office.

Military Influence

Political parties lost all their power in the government. Voters still headed to the polls to choose their representatives, but Japanese citizens knew that politics came second to the military. The biggest share of the national budget supported Japan's army and navy. As the military grew, the amount of money needed to support the military increased as well. Taxpayers may have groaned when paying their annual taxes, but Japanese citizens understood the need for a strong military to deal successfully with the rest of the world.

Prince Saionji needed to replace the newly resigned prime minister with someone who was acceptable to both the military and the politicians. The new prime minister—the third in 1937 alone—was nobleman Prince Konoe Fumimaro. Although reluctant to take the job, Konoe had the leadership skills needed to run both Japan's government and military. The new prime minister was eager to create a "national defense state" in preparation for conflict in Asia. His plans could not have been more appropriate. Konoe had been in office for only one month when the Marco Polo Bridge Incident occurred.

The Marco Polo Bridge Incident

On the evening of July 7, 1937, a company of Japanese soldiers held military exercises near the Marco Polo Bridge, not far from the Chinese city of Beijing. They used blank cartridges, firing their weapons as part of the drill. Shortly after they finished, shots rang out from a nearby Chinese encampment. After roll call, it appeared that one of the Japanese soldiers was missing. The Japanese wanted to search a nearby town for the missing soldier. The Chinese refused their request. The Japanese then attempted to enter the city by force. In the end, the lost soldier was found uninjured. In the commotion that followed the shots, the soldier had simply gotten lost.

At the time, local commanders on both the Japanese and Chinese sides had developed a working relationship. It was decided by both parties to treat the incident as unimportant because it had ended with a quiet conclusion. But when the two sides met near the bridge, however, more shots were fired toward the Japanese troops. The source of the shots was unknown.

Japan knew this was not the time to go to war with China. Japanese colonel Ishiwara Kanji, the man who planned the Manchuria Incident, had joined the army's General Staff Operation Division in Tokyo. He felt strongly that Japan could not afford to enter a prolonged war at this time. It was far more important, claimed Ishiwara, to develop a stronger military and promote economic growth in Japan. To embark on war with China was, according to Ishiwara, "the same sort of disaster which overtook Napoleon in Spain—a slow sinking into the deepest sort of bog."[32]

Soldiers stand guard on the Marco Polo Bridge, also known as the Lugou Bridge, the site of the 1937 incident that helped escalate the Sino-Japanese conflict into a full-fledged war.

80 Samurai, Shoguns, and Soldiers: The Rise of the Japanese Military

In the past, Japan had never willingly endured what they considered an insult to their national honor. In July 1937, however, saving face came second to strengthening Japan's economy and military.

The Politics of War

The local Japanese and Chinese commanders agreed to forget all about the Marco Polo Bridge Incident so their troops could get back to guarding their own lines. Their superiors, however, were not about to forgive and forget so easily. The Chinese army's headquarters in Nanjing sent additional troops to show the Japanese that the Chinese were not about to back down from a fight. The Japanese, determined not to be outdone by the Chinese, sent more troops in from Japan. The two nations stood on the brink of war, each waiting for the other to make the first move.

Japanese prime minister Konoe had no choice but to support Japan's army and its activities. After the Marco Polo Bridge Incident, "a so-called Imperial Headquarters … was set up between the army and navy to direct the war, and it became the place where the truly important national decisions were made."[33]

Chiang Kai-shek, commander of the Chinese army, decided that China needed to stand firm against the Japanese. History had shown that Japan wanted to take as much land from China as it could and would not willingly give it back. The Chinese were as nationalistic, patriotic, and prowar as the Japanese were. China had

put up with Japan's aggression in Manchuria, but now they were prepared to fight back. Chiang claimed, "If we allow one more inch of our territory to be lost, we shall be guilty of an unpardonable crime against our race."[34]

In the beginning of the war, Japan's forces quickly gained one victory after another. At home, Japanese newspapers related the news of the army's victories with pride. Only information about Japanese heroes and their exploits appeared in Japan's papers or was broadcast over the radio. The government kept a tight lid on the spread of any negative information.

Three Japanese army divisions arrived in China to bolster Japan's army in North China. In early August 1937, the Japanese marched into the Chinese city of Beijing. The Chinese retreated south to the city of Shanghai, and the battlefront spread out. Japan had only a small force of twenty-five hundred marines in Shanghai and was not prepared to fight a major battle there. The Chinese bombed the city, striking the foreign settlement in Shanghai as well as the Japanese naval station.

The Second Sino-Japanese War

Although Japan and China did not officially declare war on one another, the Second Sino-Japanese War—and World War II in Asia—was indeed underway. Japan had seriously underestimated the demands this war would place on its mil-

Mukden *v.* Marco Polo Bridge

On the surface, the Manchuria Incident of 1931 and the Marco Polo Bridge Incident of 1937 appear similar. They were both small incidents that escalated into aggressive military action. They were, however, quite different.

In 1931, the explosion that damaged train tracks outside Mukden, in Manchuria, had been set by Japan's Kwantung Army troops. The Kwantung Army had created the incident themselves merely to use it as an excuse to seize more land in Manchuria.

In 1937, Japan's army in North China did not start the Marco Polo Bridge Incident and Japan had no intention of continuing the fight.

While authorities in Japan had applauded the Manchuria Incident, they were not pleased by these current problems rising in China. In fact, they did everything in their power to repress the Marco Polo Incident and eliminate the chance of this small skirmish leading to war.

---

itary and its people. The Chinese flooded Shanghai with half a million troops, and Japan was forced to send reinforcements. Japanese troops endured three months of hand-to-hand combat and fighting in the streets of Shanghai. The Japanese won only after sending even more troops to support the weakening Japanese efforts.

The Chinese fought bravely and consistently. The Japanese were barely able to rest between battles, facing both Chiang Kai-shek's Chinese army and Communist leader Mao Zedong's guerrilla fighters. The Japanese had bragged that they would take all of China in a quick three months. They had not anticipated the resistance and determination of the Chinese troops.

In late 1937, the Japanese headed to Nanjing, which was then the capital of China. They expected to encounter Chiang Kai-shek and his army there, but Chiang Kai-shek had already left to establish a new headquarters on China's Yangtze River. Japan's general Matsui Iwane had gone to Nanjing to demonstrate to the Chinese how honorable, decent, and trustworthy the Japanese were.

In mid-December, the Japanese army entered Nanjing. Matsui claimed to have issued orders for his troops not to do anything that would dishonor Japan or Emperor Hirohito. The troops, claiming they were frustrated by the constant battles with China, erupted completely out of control. They killed not only Chinese troops but civilian men, women, and

In the mid-1930s, the population of Nanjing surpassed one million people.

children as well. Many of the Japanese believed that Chinese people were inferior to them. This racial hatred against the Chinese encouraged Japanese soldiers to act with a level of cruelty rarely seen in battle before.

The Japanese army slaughtered Chinese citizens without remorse. The Nanjing Massacre was so heinous, so brutal, that for years many Japanese refused to admit that the event had ever taken place. Between twenty thousand and eighty thousand women were attacked and murdered by Japanese soldiers. Japanese soldiers stabbed Chinese civilians with bayonets, drowned them, burned them, and shot them. The soldiers sometimes forced people to dig their own graves before shooting them with machine guns. The streets of Nanjing literally ran red with blood.

Matsui entered Nanjing in triumph, seemingly unaware of the terrible crimes committed by the Japanese army against the people of Nanjing. He said, "Now the flag of the Rising Sun is floating over Nanjing, and the Imperial Way is shining forth in the area south of the Yangtze. The dawn of the renaissance is about to take

Japanese soldiers approach the Chinese city of Tinghai in July of 1939 in an effort to tighten the blockade against Chinese shipping.

The Nanjing Massacre

In the history of war, few events have equaled the brutality and cruelty of the Nanjing Massacre. During the period from December 13, 1937, through mid-February 1938, Japanese troops ran wild through the Chinese city of Nanjing, killing, looting, and setting fire to the city. Immediately after taking the city, the Japanese army gathered ninety-eight thousand Chinese soldiers who still remained in Nanjing. The prisoners were then lined up and machine-gunned to death, beheaded, or drenched with gasoline and lit on fire. Japanese soldiers stormed through Nanjing attacking women, killing shopkeepers, and stealing whatever they wanted.

They lit buildings on fire, ignoring the cries of people locked inside them.

Twenty Americans and Europeans stayed in Nanjing during the Japanese rampage. They put up Red Cross flags to mark a safe haven in the city's center and banned the Japanese from entering. These Westerners intervened to stop murders, tortures, and other atrocities. About three hundred thousand Chinese civilians took shelter in the Red Cross zone. Another three hundred thousand Chinese died at the hands of the Japanese during this period that has come to be known as the Nanjing Massacre.

Collateral Damage

In every war, incidents occur that are not planned. Such incidents often result in collateral, or unintended, damage. In December 1937, as the Japanese advanced deeper into China, a Japanese artillery regiment fired on and seized the British ship Ladybird. The night before the army entered Nanjing, a Japanese bomb sank the USS Panay, which was anchored in China's Yangtze River. Both of these incidents were unintentional. Nonetheless, the British and U.S. governments were outraged.

The Japanese were embarrassed by these mistakes. It was bad enough that a minor incident like the one at the Marco Polo Bridge had escalated into a war with China. Japan did not want to expand its problems further by going to war with powerful Western nations like the United States and Great Britain. Japanese naval authorities dismissed the commander of their vessel responsible for the sinking of the Panay, and the Japanese government offered to pay the United States for its lost ship. Japanese foreign minister Hirota Koki issued an apology to the United States: "I am having a very difficult time. Things happen unexpectedly. ... We have [dismissed the officer responsible]."[1] The U.S. government accepted Japan's apology.

[1]John Toland, *The Rising Sun: The Decline and Fall of the Japanese Empire, 1936–1945* (New York: The Modern Library, 1970), 49.

place. On this occasion, it is my earnest hope that the four hundred million people of China will reconsider."[35] If Matsui expected the Chinese to welcome the Japanese after the crimes committed in Nanjing, he was sadly mistaken.

Matsui left Nanjing and returned to Shanghai. He remained oblivious to the truth about the behavior of Japanese soldiers in Nanjing. Despite what the Japanese people believed were major victories, Prime Minister Konoe knew that, as Ishiwara had warned, Japan's army was sinking deeper and deeper into the quicksand of war.

The Economy of War

War is expensive for governments but can be quite profitable for businesses. Soldiers need uniforms, boots, weapons, ammunition, and food. They need transportation, medicine, and payment for their services. During the fiscal year 1937–38, the Japanese government gave more than 2.5 billion yen to the military. That year, the budget for all of Japan's government

Chinese civilians watch the Zabei district of the city of Shanghai erupt in flames following another assault by Japanese bombers in November of 1937.

spending was to have been only 2.77 billion yen. Military spending in Japan was out of control.

As the war progressed, the dire predictions of Japanese officers in the General Staff came true. Japan committed more soldiers to the field, which then required more materials to support them. Japan struggled to produce the goods needed to support its troops abroad. The supply staff received orders to collect enough goods to supply fifteen army divisions in the field for a period of up to six months. The demand for materials was great, but the supply kept falling short.

The minister responsible for supply asked the government to consider an ancient concept—*gunju doin*—to ensure that factories produced the goods needed to fulfill the army's needs. Gunju doin would mean that the military would take over key industries. Most important to the war effort were factories that handled cotton, wool, wood, rubber, leather, and metal goods. Factories that produced war materials could expand, hire more workers, and earn larger profits. Businesses that only produced goods for export to other countries, however, were prohibited from expansion until the war was over.

Japanese Nationalism

With every Japanese victory, the Chinese retreated farther into the interior of China. As the Japanese army advanced, its resources became spread dangerously thin. Chiang Kai-shek's army began using a scorched earth policy, destroying absolutely everything usable on the land as they retreated. The Chinese destroyed crops, food stores, weapons, buildings, hospitals, housing, and other items that could potentially be used by the Japanese. Japan had more than seven hundred thousand men in the field. Supplying these men became nearly impossible. Despite all predictions of success, Japan was at a standstill.

This would have been a good time to negotiate peace, but neither side was willing to give up. At home, the Japanese people heard only the success stories of Japan's war with China. Negotiating a peace treaty would not make sense to the citizens who believed that Japan was clearly winning the war. Japanese newspapers labeled Chinese officials as power-hungry warlords and Communists. In the minds of the Japanese people, it had become Japan's destiny to rid their neighbors of such evil leaders.

Early in 1938, Japanese prime minister Konoe announced that he would no longer negotiate with Chinese leader Chiang Kai-shek. The only statement he was willing to hear from Chiang Kai-shek was one of surrender. Japan was now in an impossible position. There could be no retreat without losing face. There would be no victory as long as the Chinese held tight to their land.

In the fall of 1938, Japan finally captured the Chinese cities of Canton and Hankou. Konoe used this opportunity to announce a new Japanese policy in East Asia. According to Konoe, "What Japan

On October 21, 1938, Japanese soldiers celebrated their Canton victory at the entrance of the seat of the Chinese Nationalist government.

seeks is the establishment of a new order that will insure the permanent stability of East Asia. In this lies the ultimate purpose of our present military campaign."[36]

In terms of the new order, Chiang Kai-shek was considered merely a local governor with no right to speak on behalf of China as a nation. Under Japan's guidance, China would thrive, and the Chinese people would learn to appreciate the efforts Japan had made on their behalf. Japanese policy in China would demonstrate that "Japan could show mercy as well as justice. Japan was about to begin the reconstruction of China and the creation of East Asia's new order, and the [Chinese] Nationalists could join in this task."[37]

This was what the Japanese people believed. Japan was following its destiny and acting as a parent, teacher, and guide for lesser people. If Japan needed to achieve these ends through military means, so be it. For the time being, the military ran Japan and its growing empire. Emperor Hirohito, the puppet leader of the military, had little say in the actions of Japan's army and navy; the elected prime minister had even less.

As the world moved closer to joining the conflict, Japan was already under military rule. Like their shogun predecessors, the Control Faction, army generals, and navy admirals had become the true rulers of Japan. They controlled politics and policies, businesses and productivity, and even the news delivered to Japanese citizens. The concept of fukoku kyohei—rich country, strong army—had become the reality.

Notes

Chapter 1: The Early Roots of Militarism

1. "The Shogun's Order to Shimadzu *sho* concerning Tadahisa as *jito* of the sho, 1186," The Documents of Iriki (Tokyo: The University of Tokyo Historiographical Institute, 1997), http://www.hi.u-tokyo.ac.jp/iriki/eng_index.html (accessed May 11, 2007).
2. W. G. Beasley, *The Japanese Experience* (Berkeley: University of California Press, 1999), 82.
3. "Ashikaga Tadafuyu's Call for Armed Service, 1350," The Documents of Iriki (Tokyo: The University of Tokyo Historiographical Institute, 1997), http://www.hi.u-tokyo.ac.jp/iriki/eng_index.html (accessed May 11, 2007).
4. Quoted in W. G. Beasley, *The Rise of Modern Japan* (New York: St. Martin's Press, 2000), 25.
5. "President Fillmore's Letter to the Emperor of Japan," http://web.jjay.cuny.edu/~jobrien/reference/ob54.html (accessed May 11, 2007).
6. "Japanese Reply to President Fillmore's Letter," http://web.jjay.cuny.edu/~jobrien/reference/ob53.html (accessed May 11, 2007).
7. Beasley, *The Rise of Modern Japan*, 21.

Chapter 2: The Meiji Restoration

8. Quoted in Ryusaku Tsunoda, W. T. de Bary, and Donald Keene, comp., *Sources of Japanese Tradition*, vol. II (New York: Columbia University Press, 1958), 137.
9. "Waka," http://www.meijijingu.or.jp/english/intro/waka/index.htm (accessed May 21, 2007).
10. Andrew Gordon, *A Modern History of Japan: From Tokugawa Times to the Present* (New York: Oxford University Press, 2003), 66.
11. "Imperial Rescript on Education," http://www/everything2.com/index.pl?node_id=1366527 (accessed May 22, 2007).
12. Quoted in Peter Duus, *Modern Japan* (Boston: Houghton Mifflin Company, 1998), 164.
13. Ibid., 126.

Chapter 3: Times of Trouble

14. Duus, 140.
15. Prime Minister Okuma, "Japanese Prime Minister Count Okuma's Ultimatum to Germany, 15 August 1914," http://www.firstworldwar.com/source/tsingtau_okuma.htm (accessed May 11, 2007).

16. Quoted in Gordon, *A Modern History of Japan*, 158.
17. Quoted in Herbert P. Bix, *Hirohito and the Making of Modern Japan* (New York: HarperCollins Publishers, 2000), 153.

Chapter 4: Upheaval at Home and Abroad

18. Ibid., 192.
19. Quoted in Gordon, *A Modern History of Japan*, 183.
20. Quoted in Duus, *Modern Japan*, 217.
21. Gordon, *A Modern History of Japan*, 189.
22. Quoted in Bix, *Hirohito and the Making of Modern Japan*, 263.
23. Quoted in John Toland, *The Rising Sun: The Decline and Fall of the Japanese Empire, 1936–1945* (New York: The Modern Library, 1970), 12.

Chapter 5: 1936—A Pivotal Year

24. Ibid., 5.
25. Ibid., 21.
26. Quoted in "Murderous Mustards," *Time*, March 9, 1936, http://www.time.com/time/printout/o,8816,770091,00.html (accessed May 28, 2007).
27. Quoted in Toland, *The Rising Sun*, 31–32.
28. Ibid., 32.
29. Quoted in "Heroes, Dead & Alive," *Time*, July 20, 1936, http://www.time.com/time/printout/0,8816,771843,00.html (accessed May 28, 2007).

Chapter 6: The Storm Breaks

30. Quoted in "Army v. Diet," *Time*, February 1, 1937, http://www.time.com/time/printout/0,8816,788644,00.html (accessed May 29, 2007).
31. Quoted in Toland, *The Rising Sun*, 42.
32. Quoted in James L. McClain, *Japan: A Modern History* (New York: W. W. Norton & Company, 2002), 443.
33. Edwin O. Reischauer, *Japan: The Story of a Nation* (New York: McGraw-Hill Publishing Company, 1990), 164.
34. Quoted in McClain, *Japan: A Modern History*, 446.
35. Quoted in Toland, *The Rising Sun*, 50.
36. Quoted in McClain, *Japan: A Modern History*, 451.
37. Michael A. Barnhart, *Japan Prepares for Total War* (Ithaca, NY: Cornell University Press, 1987), 113.

For Further Reading

Books

Jacqueline A. Ball and Stephen Brown. *Himeji Castle: Japan's Samurai Past.* New York: Bearport Publishing, 2005. This book provides a virtual tour of one of the best examples of a Japanese castle.

Rhoda Blumberg. *Commodore Perry in the Land of the Shogun.* New York: HarperCollins Publishers, 1985. Winner of a 1986 Newbery Honor, this book describes how Matthew Perry's 1853 expedition opened Japan to foreign trade and is illustrated with reproductions of Japanese art from that time period.

Rhoda Blumberg. *Shipwrecked! The True Adventures of a Japanese Boy.* New York: HarperTrophy, 2003. This story of a fourteen-year-old Japanese boy who was shipwrecked in 1841, rescued by Americans, and returned to Japan to become an honored samurai tells the true story of the first Japanese person to set foot in the United States.

Alan M. Gratz. *Samurai Shortstop.* New York: Penguin Young Readers Group, 2006. Baseball was introduced to Japan through its contact with the United States in the late nineteenth century. This work of historical fiction tells the story of a teenage boy who tries to fit the American game into his family's samurai values.

Erik C. Haugaard. *The Samurai's Tale.* Boston: Houghton Mifflin, 2005. An adventure story set in feudal Japan, this work of fiction tells the story of a boy who sets out to become a samurai after his family is killed.

Dorothy Hoobler and Thomas Hoobler. *Showa: The Age of Hirohito.* New York: Walker & Company, 1990. This book tells the history of Japan in the twentieth century from the perspective of Emperor Hirohito.

James L. Huffman. *Modern Japan: A History in Documents.* New York: Oxford University Press, 2004. Primary documents, including picture essays, tell the story of Japan from the sixteenth century to the twenty-first century.

Katsu Kokichi. *Musui's Story: The Autobiography of a Tokugawa Samurai.* Tucson: University of Arizona Press, 1991. Katsu Kokichi was a samurai during the last decades of the Tokugawa period. His autobiography details daily life in Japan during the nineteenth century.

Inazo Nitobe. *Bushido: The Soul of Japan.* Tokyo: Kodansha International, 2002. Nitobe was a Japanese teacher in the early twentieth century who became the best-known Japanese writer in the

West during his lifetime. He wrote this book to explain Japan's virtues and values.

John R. Roberson and John Robertson. *Japan Meets the World: The Birth of a Super Power.* Minneapolis: Lerner Publishing Group, 1998. This book tells the story of Japan's history from its first contact with Portugal in the sixteenth century through the Olympics in Nagano in 1998.

Internet Sources

"An American Visit to Japan, 1923." http://www.transpect.com/japan_diary/. Read diary entries of a man who visited Japan in late summer 1923 and experienced the Great Tokyo Earthquake.

"Japan: Memoirs of a Secret Empire." http://www.pbs.org/empires/japan/. Take a virtual tour of Tokugawa Japan! Visitors explore the city of Edo through the perspectives of characters from different social classes. They can listen to music of the period or create their own woodblock print.

"Japanese Old Photographs in Bakumatsu-Meiji Period." http://oldphoto.lb. nagasaki-u.ac.jp/unive/. This site contains Nagasaki University Library's searchable database of photos taken during the years 1860–1899.

"Scenic Mementos of Japan." http://www. ndl.go.jp/site_nippon/japane/index.ht ml. This site by Japan's National Diet Library contains images of Japan from the seventeenth century through the early twentieth century.

"Visualizing Cultures." This collection by the Massachusetts Institute of Technology tells the story of Japan in the late nineteenth century and early twentieth century through a variety of images. Images are presented in exhibits, which are arranged chronologically and by topic.

Works Consulted

Books

Michael A. Barnhart. *Japan Prepares for Total War*. Ithaca, NY: Cornell University Press, 1987.

W. G. Beasley. *The Rise of Modern Japan*. New York: St. Martin's Press, 2000.

Herbert P. Bix. *Hirohito and the Making of Modern Japan*. New York: HarperCollins Publishers, 2000.

Peter Duus. *Modern Japan*. Boston: Houghton Mifflin Company, 1998.

Andrew Gordon. *A Modern History of Japan: From Tokugawa Times to the Present*. New York: Oxford University Press, 2003.

James L. McClain. *Japan: A Modern History*. New York: W. W. Norton & Company, 2002.

Edwin O. Reischauer. *Japan: The Story of a Nation*. New York: McGraw-Hill Publishing Company, 1990.

John Toland. *The Rising Sun: The Decline and Fall of the Japanese Empire, 1936–1945*. New York: The Modern Library, 1970.

Tsunoda Ryusaku, W. T. de Bary, and Donald Keene, comp. *Sources of Japanese Tradition*, vol. II. New York: Columbia University Press, 1958.

Online Periodicals

"Army v. Diet." *Time*, February 1, 1937. http://www.time.com/time/printout/0,8816,788644,00.html (accessed May 29, 2007).

"Heroes, Dead & Alive." *Time*, July 20, 1936. http://www.time.com/time/printout/0,8816,771843,00.html (accessed May 28, 2007).

"In Wake of the Quake." *Time*, September 17, 1923. http://www.time.com/time/printout/0,8816,727396,00.html (accessed May 28, 2007).

"Murderous Mustards." *Time*, March 9, 1936. http://www.time.com/time/printout/0,8816,770091,00.html (accessed May 28, 2007).

Internet Sources

"Hirohito," *Encyclopedia of World Biography*. http://www.bookrags.com/biography/hirohito (accessed May 21, 2007).

"Imperial Rescript on Education." http://www.everything2.com/index.pl?node_id=1366527 (accessed May 22, 2007).

Emperor Meiji. "Waka Poetry." http://www.meijijingu.or.jp/english/intro/waka/index.htm (accessed May 21, 2007).

"The Meiji Restoration and Moderniza-
tion." *Contemporary Japan: A Teach-
ing Workbook*. New York: Columbia
University East Asian Curriculum
Project,   2004.
http://www.afe.easia.columbia.
edu/japan/japanworkbook/modern
hist/meiji.html (accessed May 21,
2007).

"The Nanking Massacre, 1937." *Modern
History Internet Sourcebook*. http://
www.fordham.edu/halsall/mod/
nanking.html (accessed May 29, 2007).

The National Diet Library. *Modern Japan
in Archives*. http://www.ndl.go.jp/
modern (accessed May 21, 2007).

Prime Minister Okuma. "Japanese
Prime Minister Count Okuma's Ultimatum to Germany, 15 August 1914."
http://www.firstworldwar.com/source/
tsingtau_okuma.htm (accessed May
11, 2007).

"The Rape of Nanking—1937–1938—
300,000 Deaths," http://www.united
humanrights.org/nanking.htm
(accessed May 29, 2007).

Religion and Ethics—Shinto. BBC. http://
www.bbc.co.uk/religion/religions/
shinto/ (accessed May 21, 2007).

Frank E. Smitha. "Japan and Emperor
Hirohito to 1936." MacroHistory.
http://www.fsmitha.com/h2/ch18.htm
(accessed May 27, 2007).

"The Twenty-one Demands," first
worldwar.com. http://www.firstworld
war. com/atoz/21demands.htm (acc
essed May 21, 2007).

Index

Aizawa Incident, 67
Aizawa Suburo, 63–64, 67, 74
Anti-Comintern Pact, 9, 75, 77
antidraft riots, 8, 32
Ashikaga era, 19
Ashikaga Takauji, 8, 18–19
assassinations, 12, 61–64, 67, 71, 73
Austria-Hungary, 43

bakufu, 15, 18–19, 22, 25
Beijing, 39, 79, 81
black ships, 24
Buddhism, 17, 19
bushi, 15
Bushido, 10, 17, 18

Cabinet, 50, 67, 78
Canton, 87
Charter Oath of 1868, 28
Cherry Blossom Society (Sakura Kai), 57, 58, 61–63
Chiang Kai-shek, 76, 81, 82, 86, 87
China, 37
    complaints to League of Nation on Japanese aggression, 60, 61
    interests in Korea, 38
    Japanese interests in, 43, 46, 87
    Marco Polo Bridge Incident in, 9, 79–81, 82, 86
    P'u Yi as last emperor of, 60–61, 63
    rebellion in, 41
    Twenty-one Demands on, 8, 43, 45
    war with Japan, 39–40
chivalry, 10
Cho Isamu, 58

Choshu, 11, 27, 31, 36
Christianity, 21
collateral damage, 86
Comintern, 75
Communist International, 75
conscription law, 8, 31–32
conservatives, 55
Control Faction, 61, 63, 78
Council of State, 30
coup d'etat, 27, 69, 72, 73

daimyo, 13, 15, 19, 20, 23, 28, 30
Dejuna, 23
Diet, 8, 36, 43, 67, 78–79
Dutch, 20, 23
Duus, Peter, 38

East Asia
    establishment of new order in, 9, 75, 87–88
"Eastern ethics, Western science," 24
economy, 27, 33, 43–44, 46, 52, 55, 57, 65–67, 81, 86, 88
Edo, 19, 28. See also Tokyo
Edo era, 22
education, 12, 32–33
ema, 30
emperor, 13, 20
    power behind, 28, 30–31, 35–36
    privy council of, 35

factories, 34, 44, 47, 57–58, 85
farming, 34, 55, 65
    tenant, 46, 52, 55
February 26 Incident, 9, 69, 74, 75, 77, 78

feudalism, 17
Fillmore, Millard, 24–25
First shogunate, 15, 17–19
Five-Power Naval Arms Limitation Treaty, 9, 46
foreigners, expelling, 21–22
foreign trade, opening of Japan to, 8, 11, 24–26, 27, 38
France
    Five-Power Naval Arms Limitation Treaty and, 46
    as founding member of League of Nations, 45
    holdings of, 38
    recognition of Japan's rights over territory, 43
fukoku kyohei, 12, 24, 34, 36, 41, 88
Furukawa zaibatsu, 69

Gangwha, Treaty of, 38
gekokujo, 67, 69, 71–73
genro, 72
Gen'yosha (Black Ocean Society), 12
German-Japanese Anti-Comintern Pact, 9, 75, 77
Germany
    holdings of, 38
    Japanese alliance with, 77
    Japanese desire to oust from Asia, 43
    signing of Anti-Comintern Pact, 9, 75, 77
Ginza, 65, 67
Great Britain
    alliance with Japan, 41
    call on Japan, 24
    during the Second Sino-Japanese War, 86
    Five-Power Naval Arms Limitation Treaty and, 46
    as founding member of League of Nations, 45

holdings of, 38
recognition of Japan's rights over territory, 43
Great Depression, 9, 25, 52, 55, 57
Great Kanto Earthquake, 9, 46, 49

Hakodate, 25
Hamada Kunimatsu, 78
Hamaguchi Osachi, 57
Hankou, 87
hara kiri, 18, 78
Hashimoto Kingoro, 58
Hirohito, 9, 53, 74, 76, 82, 88
    death of, 74
    delay of marriage to Nagako, 49
    enthronement of, 51–52
    February 26 incident and, 72–73
    martial law and, 73–74
    as regent, 46
    scientific interests of, 74
Hiroshima, 34
Hirota Koki, 78–79, 86
Hokkaido, 34
House of Peers, 36
House of Representatives, 36
Hsinking, 60

Imperial Colors Incident, 58
Imperial Diet, see Diet
Imperialism, 12, 49
Imperial Japanese Army, 33
Imperial Middle Class Federated Alliance, 55
Imperial Rescript of Education, 32
Imperial Way, 57, 61, 83
Imperial Zone, 71
Inchon, 38
Indonesia, Japanese interests in, 46
industrialization, 33–34, 41
Industrial Revolution, 22
Inner Mongolia, 45

Inukai Tsuyoshi, 63
Ishiwara Kanji, 79
isolationist policy, 25
Italy
    Five-Power Naval Arms Limitation
        Treaty and, 46
    as founding member of League of
        Nations, 45
Ito Hirobumi, 36

Japan
    alliance with Great Britain, 41
    establishment of new order in East Asia,
        9, 75, 87–88
    export level of, 43–44
    as founding member of League of
        Nations, 8, 45
    hold over Korea, 38–43, 46
    interests in China, 43, 46, 87
    interests in Manchuria, 39
    Russia as threat to, 41, 46
    seizure of foreign territories between
        1894-1910, 42
    signing of Anti-Comintern Pact, 9, 75,
        77
    wartime boom to, from World War I, 44
    war with China, 39–40
Japanese War Office, 72–73
Japan-Korea Annexation Treaty, 41, 43

Kagoshima, 33
Kamakura, 15
Kamakura period, 15, 17
kami, 30
Kanagawa Treaty of Friendship (1854), 25
Kashii, General, 73
Keeper of the Privy Seal, 61, 69, 71
Kido Koin, 31
Kita Ikki, 67
Kodo-ha, 61
Kokuryukai (Black Dragon Society), 12

kokutai, 57, 71
Konoe Fumimaro, 79, 81, 86, 88
Korea, 38
    annexation as colony, 8, 41–43
    imperialism and, 8, 12
    Japanese hold over, 38–43, 46
    as joint territory of Japan and Russia, 41
    opening of ports to trade, 38
Kuhara zaibatsu, 69
Kwantung Army, 58, 60, 82
Kyoto, 28, 34, 52
kyuba no michi, 10

Ladybird (British ship), 86
land ownership, 13, 15, 30–31, 46, 52, 55
land-tax system, 30–31
League of Nations
    complaints on Japanese aggression to,
        60, 61
    Japan as founding member of, 8, 45
Lee Wan-Yong, 41
Liaodong Peninsula, 39, 41
Lugou Bridge, 80

Makino Nobuaki, 61
Manchukuo, 59, 60–61
Manchuria, 41, 42, 46
    Japanese interests in, 39, 41, 45
    value of, to Japan, 57–58
Manchurian Incident, 9, 58, 60, 79, 82
Mao Zedong, 82
March Incident of 1931, 58
Marco Polo Bridge Incident, 9, 79–81, 82,
    86
martial law, 73–74
Matsui Iwane, 82, 83–84
Matsuo Denzo, 69
Mazada factory, 69
Meiji, Emperor, 8, 11–12, 28, 34, 74
    death of, 8, 43
    power behind, 28–31

Meiji Constitution, 8, 34–37
Meiji Restoration, 27–37, 41, 69
men, military service of, 12
militarism, 46, 49–50, 86
    assassinations and, 61–64
    roots of, 10, 12, 13–26
military
    Control Faction of, 61, 63, 78
    discipline in, 49
    influence of, 79
    limitations on size of, 46, 49
    need for strong, 79
    needs of, 84–85
    power of, 31–32
    reorganization of, 46, 49
Minamoto era, 15
Minamoto family, 8, 15, 17–18
Minamoto Yorimoto, 8, 15, 17
Minseito (Democratic) Party, 57
Mitsubishi, 69
Mitsui, 69
Mitsui Bank, 69
Mommu, Emperor, 10
Mukden, 58, 82
munitions industry, 34
Muromachi, 19
Muromachi period, 8, 19
mustards, 71
Mutsuhito, Prince, 27–28

Nagako, Princess, delay of marriage, 49
Nagasaki, 20, 23
Nagata Tersuzan, 67
Nagato, 19
Nagoya, 34
Nanjing, 81, 82–84
Nanjing Massacre, 9, 82, 84
National Bank of Japan, 69
nationalism, 12, 25, 28, 32, 43, 49–50, 57,
    61, 86–88
New York Stock Market, crash of, 9, 52

Nonaka Shiro, 73

Okada Keisuke, 69–71, 72
Okura zaibatsu, 69
oligarchy, 28, 35
Omura Masujiro, 31
Oriental renegades, 38
Osaka Castle, 20
Osaka Spinning Company, 34

patriotic societies, 12, 57
patriotism, 12, 63
Perry, Matthew, 8, 11, 24–25, 38
Pescadores Islands, 39
political slogans, 36
population, 34, 65
Prefectures, 30
privy council, 35
Pusan, 38
P'u Yi, 60–61, 63, 76

Qing dynasty, 63

radicals, 55
regents, 46
rice riots, 45
Russia
    call on Japanese ports, 24
    interest in Korea, 41
    threat to Japan, 41, 46
Russo-Japanese War, 41

Saigo Takamori, 33
Saionji Kinmochi, 69, 78, 79
Sakuma Shozan, 24
Sakura Kai (Cherry Blossom Society), 57,
    58, 61–63
samurai, 8, 10, 11, 12, 13, 15, 16, 17–18, 27
    code of behavior for, 33
    losing face by, 18
    sense of honor of, 22–23

wealth of, 20
samurai sword, 16
sankin-kotai system, 19
Satsuma, 11, 27, 33, 36
Satsuma Rebellion, 8, 33
scorched earth policy, 86
second shogunate, 18–19
Sekigahara, battle at, 19
seppuku, 18, 33, 73
Shandong Peninsula, 45
Shanghai, 81–82
    burning of Zabei district in, 87
Shibusawa Eiichi, 34
Shimoda, 25
Shimonoseki, Treaty of, 39–40
Shinto, 30
Shishi soldiers, 25, 26
shogunates, 15, 30, 31
    first, 15, 17–19
    second, 18–19
shoguns, 8, 10, 13, 15, 17, 20, 26
Showa era, 9, 74
Sino-Japanese War
    first, 8
    second, 9, 81–84
social pyramid, 20, 24
sonno joi, 26, 36
Southern Manchuria Railroad, 41
Stalin, Joseph, 76
Sumitomo, 69

Tadafuyu, 19
Tadayoshi, 19
Taisho Emperor, 51, 74
    death of, 9, 51
Taisho era, 41, 43, 46
Taiwan, 39, 42
Takauji, 19
Tanaka Giichi, 49
taxes, 15, 30–31
teacher training schools, 32

tenant farmers, 46, 52, 55, 57
Terauchi Masaki, 45
textile industry, 34
timeline, 8–9
Tinghai, 85
Tokugawa, 24
Tokugawa era, 8, 19, 21–22, 26, 27
Tokugawa Ieyasu, 8, 19
Tokyo, 8, 9, 19, 41, 52
    Ginza in, 65, 67
    Great Kanto Earthquake and, 46, 49
Tokyo Bay, 11
Tosei-ha, 61
trade unions, 67
    women as members of, 47
trading rights, establishment of, 8, 11,
    24–26, 27, 38
Tsingtao, Japanese capture of, 43, 44
Twenty-one Demands, 8, 43, 45

Ugaki Kazushige, 58, 78
ultranationalism, 25–26
unemployment, 55
United States
    Five-Power Naval Arms Limitation
        Treaty and, 46
    foreign trade with Japan, 8, 11, 24, 27, 38
    holdings of, 38
    recognition of Japan's rights over terri-
        tory, 43
USS Panay, 86

waka poetry, 28
women, 18, 67
    working conditions of, 34, 47
Wonsan, 38
World War I, 8, 43–44
    impact on Japan, 44–45
    Japan's participation in, 44
World War II, 60, 74, 81
    Japanese surrender at end of, 63

Yamagata Aritomo, 31
Yangtze River, 82, 83, 86
Yasuda family, 69
Yasukuni Shrine, 11
Yellow Sea, 39

Yokohama, 9, 34, 52
   Great Kanto Earthquake and, 46, 49
Yoshihito, Emperor, 43

zaibatsu, 52, 67, 69

Picture Credits

Cover photo: Hulton Archive/Getty Images
AFP/Getty Images, 14, 23, 83, 85, 89
DAJ/Getty Images, 20
Hulton Archive/Getty Images, 11, 29, 39, 44, 48, 50, 54, 56, 62, 87
Rekidai Shusho tou Shashin/National

Diet Library Archives, Tokyo, 70
Retrofile/Getty Images, 66
Time & Life Pictures/Getty Images, 17, 35, 40, 53, 72, 76, 80
Roger Viollet/Getty Images, 47, 68
Adrian Weinbrecht/Stone/Getty Images, 16

About the Author

Barbara A. Somervill writes children's nonfiction books on a wide range of topics. She is particularly interested in nature and foreign cultures because the research provides so much new information. All this new knowledge makes writing every book an adventure. Her favorite writing projects so far have been biographies of Abigail Adams and Eleanor Roosevelt and a series of books on biomes. When she is not writing, Ms. Somervill is an avid reader and plays duplicate bridge.

About the Consultant

Dr. David Tobaru Obermiller is an assistant professor at University of Wisconsin, Superior.